HADRIAN'S WALL PATH
NATIONAL TRAIL

ABOUT THE AUTHOR

Mark Richards' transition from full-time farmer to full-time outdoor writer has been a gradual one. In 1973, with the direct encouragement of Alfred Wainwright, he wrote his first walking guide to the Cotswold Way. Since then he has indulged his pleasure in exploring rural Britain by creating a range of walking guides.

In 1980 he began his three-part guide to the Peak District for Cicerone Press, and in 1987, with Chris Wright, wrote a guide to walking around the former county of Westmorland. This book sowed the seeds of a dream, to be fulfilled some 14 years later, when he and his wife moved to Cumbria. Here he developed a passion for the finest of all walking landscapes, held within and around this marvellous county.

Now, living in what was once the Barony of Gilsland, Mark is close to Hadrian's Wall, enabling him to renew a fascination first kindled when he prepared a guide to walking the Wall in 1993.

HADRIAN'S WALL PATH NATIONAL TRAIL

Walk the Roman Frontier

by

Mark Richards

CICERONE

2 POLICE SQUARE, MILNTHORPE, CUMBRIA LA7 7PY
www.cicerone.co.uk

© Mark Richards, 2004
ISBN 1 85284 392 6

A catalogue record for this book is available from the British Library.

 HARVEY The sketch maps reproduced here are based upon
Harvey's map services' *Hadrian's Wall Path Map*

Dedication

This guide is dedicated to my wife, Helen, for her perseverance in establishing
the Hadrian's Wall Path Trust and setting a firm course for its long-term future.

Acknowledgements

My thanks for much appreciated advice from: Paul Austen, Jane Brantom, Carol
Donnelly, Dennis Frazer, Raymond Hunneysett, Steve Hunneysett, David
McGlade, Rachel Newman, Helen Richards, Elaine Watson and Geoff
Woodward, but particularly to Paul Beniams for his insatiable enthusiasm for the
Wall and the fun times we have had together.

Advice to Readers

Readers are advised that whilst every effort is taken by the author to ensure the
accuracy of this guidebook, changes can occur which may affect the contents. A book
of this nature, with detailed descriptions and maps, is more prone to change than a
general travel guide. New fences and stiles appear, waymarking alters, and there may
be new buildings or eradication of old buildings. It is advisable to check locally on
transport, accommodation, shops, etc, but even rights of way can be altered and paths
eradicated by landslip, forest clearance and changes in land ownership. The publisher
would welcome notes of any such changes for future editions.

Front cover: Crag Lough from Castle Nick

CONTENTS

Appendices

HADRIAN'S WALL PATH   134 km/84 miles

Solway Coast AONB

BOWNESS-ON-SOLWAY
Maia

PORT CARLISLE

DRUMBURGH
Congavata

DUMFRIES & GALLOWAY

Aballava

BURGH-BY-SANDS

BEAUMONT

Scotland

CARLISLE
Luguvalium

GRINSDALE

Petriana - Uxelodunum

LINSTOCK

CROSBY-ON-EDEN

ALL THE MAPS IN
THIS GUIDE SHOW
WEST AT THE TOP
OF THE PAGE

NEWTOWN

Camboglanna

WALTON

CUMBRIA

BRAMPTON

BANKS

☐	Wall Forts
☐	Stanegate Forts

North Pennines
Area of Outstanding
Natural Beauty

Banna

GILSLAND

GREENHEAD

Magna

NORTHUMBERLAND

HALTWHISTLE

Northumberland
National Park

Aesica

BARDON MILL

Vindolanda

Vercovicium

HAYDON BRIDGE

Brocolitia

England

NEWBROUGH

Cilurnum

WALL

CHOLLERFORD

HEXHAM

NORTHUMBERLAND

Corstopitum

CORBRIDGE

Onnum

NORTH

PRUDHOE

HARLOW HILL

WYLAM

Vindovala

TYNE AND WEAR

RYTON

HEDDON-ON-THE-WALL

NEWBURN

BLAYDON

Condercum

GATESHEAD

Pons Aelius

NEWCASTLE-
UPON-TYNE

WALLSEND Segedunum

KEY TO THE SKETCH MAPS

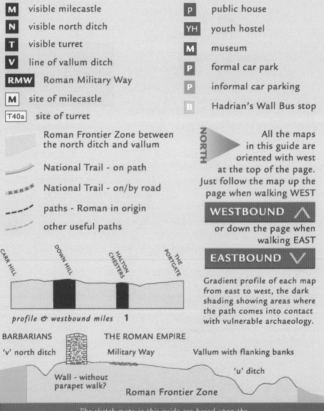

M	visible milecastle
N	visible north ditch
T	visible turret
V	line of vallum ditch
RMW	Roman Military Way
M	site of milecastle
T40a	site of turret

Roman Frontier Zone between the north ditch and vallum

National Trail - on path

National Trail - on/by road

paths - Roman in origin

other useful paths

P	public house
YH	youth hostel
M	museum
P	formal car park
P	informal car parking
B	Hadrian's Wall Bus stop

NORTH

All the maps in this guide are oriented with west at the top of the page. Just follow the map up the page when walking WEST

WESTBOUND ∧

or down the page when walking EAST

EASTBOUND ∨

Gradient profile of each map from east to west, the dark shading showing areas where the path comes into contact with vulnerable archaeology.

CARR HILL · DOWN HILL · HALTON CHESTERS · THE PORTGATE

profile & westbound miles **1**

BARBARIANS — 'v' north ditch — THE ROMAN EMPIRE — Military Way — Vallum with flanking banks

Wall - without parapet walk?

'u' ditch

Roman Frontier Zone

The sketch maps in this guide are based upon the
HARVEY National Trail Map

INTRODUCTION

HADRIAN'S WALL: INSPIRED AND INSPIRING

The creation of Hadrian's Wall was the master-stroke of Emperor Hadrian Aelius, who thereby achieved two things all rulers dream of – contemporary acclaim and lasting renown. Constructed purely for military reasons, the Wall endured as an effective frontier for almost 300 years. The cultural significance of Hadrian's Wall, the finest surviving frontier work from any part of the classical Roman Empire, was recognised in 1987 when it was designated a UNESCO World Heritage Site.

Hadrian's startling idea was to string out a wall from coast to coast:

Emperor Hadrian

predominantly constructed of stone, this linear divide ran 84 miles (134km) from the tidal Tyne at Newcastle in the east to the Solway Firth, west of Carlisle. Such a monumental departure from existing

Hadrian's Wall on Walltown Crags (18/15)

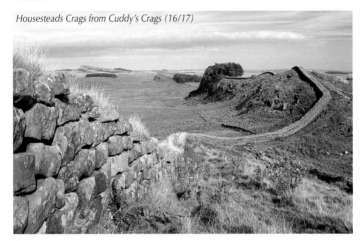

Housesteads Crags from Cuddy's Crags (16/17)

Roman thinking was quite simply inspired. He may have seen, and been influenced by the great pyramids of Egypt. But he is unlikely to have known that the Emperor of China had lighted upon the same solution some four centuries earlier to quell Mongol tribes to the north of that great empire.

Hadrian came to power in AD117 and inherited a volatile situation at the northern edge of his empire. After failed attempts under Governor Agricola to conquer Scotland, Rome had established a frontier road between the Tyne and the Solway Firth. Two important forts at Corbridge and Carlisle were linked by a road now known as the Stanegate, and additional forts were built along its east–west route. Hadrian's innovation was to replace the Stanegate with a physical frontier – a defensible line of control that interrupted the erratic movement

of the Celtic tribes which so troubled the Romans. As Hadrian's biographer put it 'the Wall was to separate the Romans from the barbarians' (the term 'barbarian' comes from the Greek for a primitive and uncivilised people).

The Wall appeared to be the perfect 'grand scheme' to enhance Hadrian's standing at the helm of the Roman Empire. However, as the only stone-built frontier in the history of the empire, it also represented a seismic change in thinking – as the usual timber structures of an expanding empire were replaced by a permanent frontier that suggested a policy of inward-looking containment. If the Wall was a tacit acknowledgement of the end of the hitherto limitless expansion of the Roman Empire, this was not the intention of the flamboyant Hadrian. To him, the Wall was a statement of authority, not an admission that the empire had reached its limit ('limit' comes from the Roman word 'limes', meaning 'a frontier').

Although the frontier played an active part in Roman life for nearly three centuries, once Roman jurisdiction fell away the Wall lost its meaning too. Remarkably the Wall remained largely intact for the next 1000 years, mainly because local buildings were predominantly timber-built. Its only enemy was the damp northern climate and the occasional monastic 'borrowing'. Later, when most buildings came to be made of stone, it was open season on the long-defunct frontier, and farmers and house-builders took the stones in cart-loads.

That there is any trace of the Wall remaining today is largely due to the enlightened and prompt action of one man, John Clayton of Chesters, whose estate was located some five miles north of Hexham, just west of Chollerford, where the Wall crossed the North Tyne. At the end of the 18th century Clayton's father began to turn his country seat into a fashionable stately park, and in the process virtually flattened Roman Cilurnum. However, upon inheriting the estate in 1822 Clayton began reversing this process: his classical education served him particularly well, for he realised the importance of the Roman site in the grounds and developed a passion for the frontier with which it was associated. Clayton then proceeded to acquire farm after farm along the line of the

Wall as far as the Cumberland border (present day Cumbria), thus abruptly ending the thoughtless pilfering of Wall-stone.

BUILDING THE WALL

With typical Roman military directness, Hadrian's Wall forms an almost straight east–west divide, crossing the narrowest neck or isthmus of the most northerly Roman province, Britannia, from Segedunum in Wallsend (GR NZ 240640) to Maia at Bowness-on-Solway (GR NY 400560).

Building the Wall was no mean feat, as it required some two million tons of stone to be cut, hauled and laid to create a curtain wall of stone, with turf and timber sections also being built on the west of the Irthing. The main work was concentrated in a 10-year period from AD122, and was undertaken by three legions: XX Valeria, VI Victrix and II Augusta.

The Wall had integrated **forts** approximately every five miles, garrisoned by cavalry or foot soldiers. There were also frontier post gates every mile, built into what are now termed **milecastles** (there is no record of their Roman name nor of how each was distinguished, hence the latterday sequential numbering system for the milecastles). A small detachment of auxillary soldiers would have been billeted at the milecastle to perform border control duties. Observation towers featured every $1/3$ mile (Roman mile) between the milecastles.

Hadrian's Wall above Thorny Doors

Milecastles were set at 1620 yard intervals. Without the aid of cartography, Romans must have judged distances by marching from one place to another. The Roman mile (Latin 'mille', from which we derive the word 'mile') was equivalent to 1000 marching paces (double-steps).

On the south side of the Wall a **military way** or supply road ran close by, and a double-banked ditch (termed the **vallum**) was created at varying distances further to the rear of the Wall. A **'v' ditch** was constructed immediately north of the Wall, so the the area from the north ditch to the

Voices from the Past

Throughout the walk you will encounter intriguing 'born-again' Roman names on modern road signs for various sites, such as Segedunum and Vindolanda. The original Roman names of most sites along the Wall have been deduced and brought back into currency. If only we knew what they called the other constituent features – the milecastles, turrets and so on – we would have an even better understanding of the frontier from a Roman vernacular perspective.

One magical window on the past is found in the Vindolanda 'Writing Tablets', which alone make this site an absolute 'must visit' place. The tablets give a sneak glimpse into the daily conversations of the Roman garrison and their families in the period leading up to the building of the Wall (AD80–122).

vallum became, at a stroke, an exclusive military zone that separated the civil order of the empire from the barbarian territory to the north.

Specifications for the Wall underwent various modifications during the 10 years it took to build. At the outset, the plan was for a stone wall some 10 Roman feet thick (known as the **Broad Wall**) and perhaps 15 feet high running from Newcastle to the River Irthing, with a turf wall completing the journey to the coast at Bowness-on-Solway. The turf wall was 20 Roman feet thick at its base, set on stable bed of cobbles, and was a solution to the

Looking east from Birdoswald

DIVIDE AND RULE

Movement north and south through the Wall was regulated; tolls may have been exacted; and groups or individuals passing through the frontier were possibly forced to exit some distance east or west of their point of entry thus further disrupting established patterns of movement. The Wall was like a motorway driven through an ancient wood, which suddenly cuts animals off from their established territory and disrupts their social patterns; the Celtic Brigantes tribe experienced a similar dislocation.

logistical problems of hauling stone some distance and to the lack of lime available for mortar. Later the turf wall was replaced by a stone wall.

The logistics of building a 10-foot Broad Wall appear to have caused a rethink. An early change, narrowing the basic wall from a 10- to an 8-foot width, was undertaken partly to save time – as the construction process was carried out amid the constant threat of terror raids from not unnaturally disgruntled Celts. While the Wall foundations and look-out turrets were being set in place, the process of westward wall-building changed at Planetrees on the east side of the North Tyne valley; here we see the start of the 8-foot-wide **Narrow Wall**.

The Wall has often been portrayed with a castellated parapet walk on top to match those on the forts, milecastles and turrets. This seems unlikely, as the forts and milecastles had viewing towers, which quickly rendered even the turrets obsolete.

The **vallum** appears to have been an early invention to broaden the area of military control, though, like the

turrets, which were uniformly demolished, it seems to have quickly lost its value, and crossings were constructed over it that negated its original function. (See key to sketch map.)

Where the Wall crossed major streams and rivers fine **bridges** were built, and were later enhanced with what might be termed 'chariot ramps' to service the speedy movement of cavalry and marching men.

The many subtle details of the Wall frontier – its phases, along with the various individual layouts of the forts, milecastles and turrets, and the daily life of garrisons and auxiliaries – are not given here as they are generally well displayed either on site, in nearby museums or in the excellent publications of English Heritage and others (see bibliography).

The Builders

Fifteen thousand men from three legions – XX Valeria, VI Victrix and II Augusta – were employed on the task of building the Wall, and no doubt there was a certain rivalry between the legions.

Building of the Wall, milecastles and turrets was strictly standardised from the outset, though interpretation of the rules allowed for a certain level of individuality. Inscribed stones were built into the Wall at regular intervals to indicate which legion or cohort built that section – they were simultaneously a tribute to the honour of the empire and an indication of pride in a job well done.

Some indication of 'who built what' can also be deduced from the size of the various milecastles. Studies suggest (see bibliography) that the following three legions constructed the majority of milecastles:

- **XX Valeria** (milecastles 18, 19, 22, 29, 30, 44, 45, 53, 54)
- **VI Victrix** (9, 10, 23, 27, 33, 34, 35, 36, 39, 40, 50)
- **II Augusta** (13, 14, 17, 37, 38, 41, 42, 43, 52).

THE WALL TODAY

The following terms are used in this guide to describe the various states in which the Wall exists today.

Consolidated Wall: sections where English Heritage has rebuilt the structure with mortar to resist the elements for long-term outdoor exhibition.

Clayton Wall: dry-stone reconstruction with turf on top, conducted under the instructions of John Clayton of Chesters House in the 19th century. This Wall is prone to periodic collapse and repair; walkers clambering onto it have been the main culprits of this decay – please, please keep off.

Semi-field Wall: many instances of genuine remnant Wall linger as small base sections of field-wall or as random individual stones – there's a sport in trying to spot them.

Rubble Rigg: in areas where most of the good masonry has been stolen, sad linear mounds remain *in situ*. These unexcavated lengths still need securing for the long-term and are just as important as more obvious Wall sections.

In some places, there is no tangible trace of the Wall – its former existence indicated only by the line of an enclosure field-wall, hedge or fence. At other times it runs across open pasture, under houses and even under tarmac! (The one saving grace is that the tarmac is protecting the foundations and could be lifted.) One of the best stretches of Wall, though it does not replicate the wall and is not in situ, is that reused as part of the bounding enclosure to Lanercost Priory, Cumbria. This medieval rebuild is about one-third of the height of the original Wall.

A WORLD HERITAGE SITE

In 1987 Hadrian's Wall became a UNESCO World Heritage Site. The site is not only the best preserved of all the Roman Empire's frontiers, it is also the most complex. As well as encompassing the remains of Hadrian's Wall itself (ie. the stone structure, with its forts, milecastles and turrets) from Segedunum in Wallsend to Maia at Bowness-on-Solway, the site includes:

- Arbeia, the coastal fort at South Shields at the mouth of the River Tyne
- numerous structures and features including the north ditch, the vallum and the counterscarp mound
- civilian settlement sites (*vicii*)
- Roman quarry sites (eg. Combe Crag)
- the Stanegate (which came into being around the mid-80s AD, from which date there was a continued Roman presence in the area), with its attendant forts south of the line of the Wall, most famously Vindolanda
- outpost scouting forts such as that at Bewcastle
- various defences down the Cumbrian coast by Maryport as far south as the Roman port at Ravenglass.

HADRIAN'S WALL PATH NATIONAL TRAIL

The establishment of a continuous trail along Hadrian's Wall has been suggested since Clayton's time as scholars, the inquisitive and, later, a more leisured society rediscovered this relic from classical times. They wanted to visit it, to sense and to see the monument in its entirety and in the fullness of its setting.

Hotbank Farm backed by Crag Lough (16/17)

Clayton Wall on Hotbanks Crags (16/17)

The establishment of a similar trail accompanying the later Saxon divide of Offa's Dyke in 1971 did nothing to hasten the arrival of its northern counterpart. However, Hadrian's Wall Path National Trail was opened some 30 years later in May 2003 – marking a harmony of purpose between the Countryside Agency and English Heritage. It stretches a total of 84 miles (134km) from Wallsend (Segedunum) in the east to Bowness-on-Solway in the west.

Great efforts have been made to keep the trail close to the line of the Wall itself. There are a few short steep gradients in the central Whin Sill section – some have stone flag-steps, as do places where the path briefly crosses marshy ground. At either end the trail is composed almost exclusively of unforgiving tarmac, but the predominant surface is a green sward. Throughout, the gradients and nature of the path encourage a flowing stride, making this an excellent exercise for anyone of normal fitness and a fine warm-up for something more adventurous.

There is no charge made to walk the path, which takes the walker past a string of fascinating Roman and later historic sites, each in turn furthering one's understanding of the context of the walk. Of these sites, English Heritage owns Chesters, Aydon Castle, Corbridge, Housesteads, Birdoswald, Lanercost Priory and Carlisle Castle; Segedunum and Arbeia belong to Tyne & Wear Museums; the Museum of Antiquities belongs to the University of Newcastle; Tullie House Mueum to Carlisle City Council; and Vindolanda and Carvoran are privately owned. There are charges for entry to all these sites (an English Heritage membership card is valuable).

Cawfields Quarry (17/16)

Protecting the Trail and the Wall

The arrival of the trail is but one more instance of change for the Wall, which over the past 20, 50 or 100 years has seen its close environs more than cosmetically changed. The route is attracting many people new to the notion of walking a long distance path, and the pressure of a myriad boots upon a vulnerable archaeology has the obvious potential for adverse impact.

For generations people have wandered freely along the Wall. However, the number of people visiting the Wall today makes it necessary to protect

this vulnerable environment – hopefully without sullying the experience for visitors. In recognition of the fact that this is a World Heritage Site route, which requires a different approach from a normal National Trail, the Countryside Agency have instituted a two-season system, operated through the use of Summer and Winter Passports (booklets).

The Summer Passport (1st May to end of October) scheme offers walkers the chance to have their passport stamped at six points along their coast-to-coast walk – at Segedunum, Robin Hood Inn, Chesters, Birdoswald, Sands Centre in Carlisle and The Banks in Bowness-on-Solway. The Winter Passport (1st November to end of April) provides stamping posts located off the line of the National Trail and therefore away from the vulnerable sections of Wall. These points are associated with a number of circular walks designed to illustrate the bigger picture of the Hadrian's Wall corridor.

To stem erosion – the enemy of this vulnerable monument – a small rack structure (termed a 'tank trap') is being inserted into sections of the Path that are showing signs of wear. These should encourage walkers to veer onto a new line and thus preserve the site.

At the time of going to press the Winter Passport points had yet to be determined; they may vary from season to season to give new emphasis both scenically and in terms of trade for local businesses. For further information about the Passport booklets and the Trail see www.nationaltrail .co.uk/hadrianswall

WORLD HERITAGE SITE AND THE RESPONSIBLE WALKER

'Every Footstep Counts', a voluntary code of practice for walkers and other visitors to this World Heritage Site, has been devised to protect the trail and the Wall itself. Hadrian's Wall is the only World Heritage Site in the UK to have such a code. National Trail walkers can contribute to the conservation and general well-being of Hadrian's Wall by following the points below.

1. During the wet winter months the ground becomes waterlogged and the risk of damage to the monument from walkers' feet is greatest. When this is the case, please respect the archaeology. Instead, consider visiting a Roman site or walking one of the many shorter circular walks along the Wall's corridor – specific routes are identified in the Winter Passport Scheme, with special stamping posts off the line of the National Trail.

2. If you are walking only a part of the trail, consider starting your walk at places that are not stage starts or follow a circular route. By doing so, the amount of wear and tear to the path will be reduced.

3. Keep off the Wall. The one exception to this rule is a public right-of-way on top of the Wall in Housesteads Wood, though even here an alternative path winds more sympathetically through the pine coppice.

4. Help to take pressure off the Wall itself by exploring one of the excavated Roman forts. Such forts have facilities and excellent interpretative displays.

5. Only walk along the signed and waymarked paths, and where a so-called 'tank trap' (small wooden structure) has been set on the line of the path, heed its advice.

6. Keep your dog on a lead wherever loose stock are near the trail: this is compulsory on National Trust property.

7. Take your litter away with you and never light fires.

8. Close all gates behind you unless it is clear that the farmer needs the gate to be left open.

9. Hadrian's Wall is a scheduled ancient monument. Play your part in ensuring that it remains intact for future generations to appreciate and enjoy.

HADRIAN'S WALL PATH TRUST

The Hadrian's Wall Path Trust was founded in 2004. This 'watchdog' organisation aims to speak up for the Hadrian's Wall Path and the World Heritage Site with the aim of giving them a sustainable future and preserving them for subsequent generations.

The Trust has published *The Essential Guide to Hadrian's Wall Path National Trail*, prepared by David McGlade, the National Trail Officer. Based on questions and requests he received from walkers, this reference book gives important information about services and amenities in the area. It is updated annually. £1 from every copy sold goes towards the trail. The book is available from Tourist Information Centres and most Roman Wall sites within the World Heritage Site, or by mail order from the Hadrian's Wall Information Line, tel: 01434 322 002.

For the latest news on the Trust and details of membership please check the National Trails website at: www.nationaltrail.co.uk/hadrianswall

USING THIS GUIDE

People walk the trail in both directions, though the westbound route is always likely to attract the greater number. Not only was it the way the Wall was built, but it is the most rewarding. Escaping the urban environment of Tyneside, with all its majestic architecture and historical significance, the trail heads via the great Whin Sill ridge, heading always towards the setting sun which, at the end of the last day's walk, streaks golden light across the Solway Firth. The small matter of having a prevailing wind in one's face on occasion is a minor distraction.

To accommodate both west- and eastbound walkers, the guide divides the trail into 32 sections (each begins and ends where a car may appropriately be parked) that describe the route in both directions. The route

In recognition of the pre-eminence, uniqueness and vulnerability of Hadrian's Wall World Heritage Site, the Trust's aims.

• to promote the recreational and educational value of the National Trail in a way that is archaeologically, environmentally and economically sustainable

• to provide a forum for visitors and locals alike, indeed anyone with an interest in the trail, to contribute ideas and enthusiasm towards the long-term well-being of both the World Heritage Site and its Path

• to lobby national/local government, business/organisation or individual in order to achieve these aims

number itself is composed of two parts – the first applies to the west-bound route; the second to the eastbound. Each section first sets out the westbound route in detail, then provides a shorter summary of the eastbound route. A route summary is given in Appendix 2.

The maps in the guide are designed to make it easier to appreciate where one is from the trail's perspective, hence west is consistently to the top of the page.

> Follow the sketch map up the page when walking **westbound**.
>
> Alternatively, follow the map down the page when walking **eastbound**.

They are sketch maps, intended to keep matters simple for quick reference. To help with orientation, the main landmarks on the sketch maps are indicated in **bold** in the text.

Walkers should always take the relevant conventional map(s) with them. Details of maps needed for the trail are set out in the bibliography. The Hadrian's Wall area is blessed with all manner of really good literature, including excellent maps.

PLANNING A COAST-TO-COAST WALK

Too many people who contemplate walking Hadrian's Wall Path over-estimate their capacity and under-estimate the task. The key word here is planning. The Path may only be 84 miles long, and for much of its course it passes over comparatively gently contoured country. But there are major pitfalls for anyone new to walking successive days to a tight schedule.

Where to begin? Well, Arbeia (pronounced R-bay-A) at South Shields, a Roman supply port and fort at the mouth of the Tyne, has much to reward the visitor and thoroughly merits a visit from anyone genuinely interested in seeing as much of the Wall frontier system as possible. A leaflet is available describing a seven-mile walking route via Jarrow and the Tyne Foot Tunnel, built in 1948 for shipyard workers. However, experience suggests many walkers will be

> It is imperative for your own enjoyment and convenience to plan your visit carefully in advance. Consult the guide produced by the Hadrian's Wall Tourism Partnership (for accommodation) and the *Essential Guide to Hadrian's Wall*, published by the Hadrian's Wall Path Trust (for practical advice). These are both updated annually. Also helpful is the Hadrian's Wall Information Line, tel: 01434 322002; email haltwhistle@ btconnect.com.

Hadrian's Wall Bus at Birdoswald (20/13)

content with a firm schedule set upon the National Trail, and choose Segedunum as their starting point.

Two pieces of advice for the first day – wear lightweight boots or trainers, and allow yourself a chance to get into the pattern of walking day after day. Start steadily – the stretch of Path from Wallsend to the Tyne Riverside Country Park at Newburn is unrelenting tarmac (19km/12 miles). While some folk, used to hard surfaces, may think nothing of it, I suggest the majority will rue their folly should they not heed their feet early on. Be prepared, at the first hint of soreness, to ring a change – slip on a barrier plaster, different socks or footwear, placing the emphasis on a different area of the sole. If you allow your feet to form blisters they will spoil the whole walk.

For accommodation, some walkers (the more hardy type) use camping and camping barn facilities. Although at present there is a paucity of this type of accommodation, the situation is improving. The majority choose the greater comforts of B&B, savouring the good food and wider scenic delights of the area. Again, there are stretches with insufficient B&B accommodation to meet the high-season demand, and walkers who set out without pre-booking can find they have unexpected taxi bills to get them to and from a more distant lodging.

Appendices 1 and 2 list organisations and publications that can provide information on accommodation, etc, that will help you to plan your walk.

Remember you are here for pleasure, to sense the magic of walking coast to coast with history at your very feet. Why not include a circular walk; take a proper look at nearby sites and towns; or, with this being a trail of two cities, make time to really explore Newcastle and Carlisle?

Too many walkers treat the sections from Gilsland to Carlisle and then Carlisle to Bowness as one-day marches because of apparent deficiencies in the chain of accommodation. This is most unfortunate and probably unnecessary if you undertake a bit of forward planning. The best overall approach, on the basis that most walkers embark at a weekend, is to start on a weekday. The benefits of this strategy become clear when you reach the middle section of the route, where competition for beds is most intense. You will be a day or two behind the bulk of walkers and therefore stand a better chance of finding that much appreciated pillow. One of the problems of a hugely popular route with finite accommodation is that, to ensure solid bookings, many B&Bs tie in with tour operators and block-book, making it almost impossible to find an impromptu bed for the night near the path in high season.

The common itinerary for the Path is for a seven-day traverse, but I would be falling short of my praise of this historic and scenic corridor to recommend anything less than nine to ten days as the most rewarding plan. A sensibly measured ten-day schedule,

that will reward you long after the experience itself is over is listed on the next page. This schedule is not a fixed plan – you must do the walk your way. As a further valuable device, in support of sustainable tourism, why not determine to stay a minimum of two nights at each lodging, using a taxi or Hadrian's Wall bus for continuity (see 'Bus to Bus', below)?

Segedunum fort and museum (1/32)

DAY 1 – Segedunum (with lunch-time stroll in Newcastle) to Newburn (westbound sections 1–4)

DAY 2 – Newburn to Harlow Hill (sections 5–6)

DAY 3 – Harlow Hill to Portgate (sections 7–9)

DAY 4 – (with morning visit to *Corstopitum*) Portgate to Chollerford (sections 10–11)

DAY 5 – Chollerford to Housesteads (sections 12–15)

DAY 6 – Housesteads (with mid-day visit to *Vindolanda*) to Cawfields (sections 16–17)

DAY 7 – Cawfields to Gilsland (sections 18–19)

DAY 8 – Gilsland to Crosby-on-Eden (sections 20–25)

DAY 9 – Crosby-on-Eden (with a look around Carlisle) to Grinsdale (sections 26–27)

DAY 10 – Grinsdale to Bowness-on-Solway (sections 28–32)

(A complete route summary is given in Appendix 2.)

BE PREPARED

While an army may march on its stomach, a long-distance walker relies on his or her head – thinking in advance what may be needed when far from base. The Roman scouts had to be protected against the uncertainties of the northern climate, and you should be similarly prepared for exposure to wind, rain and intense sun. Walkers should be aware that comfort facilities are frequently unavailable en route – there are considerable stretches where one would have to leave the path to find toilet facilities, drinks, food or shelter. Walkers need to carry their own resources to avoid such discomforts, and in this day and age there are lightweight options available. It is only drinks that are an unavoidable weight.

For up-to-date information on refreshments and other facilities consult the Hadrian's Wall Path Trust's *Essential Guide* (see bibliography).

WALKING THE TRAIL PIECEMEAL

Many people do not walk the Path in one go, but in measured portions – frequently either 'there and back' – or by making circular walks. But there are other ways.

'Two-car Trick'

Taking two cars on a walk may seem to be a bit of an indulgence, but frequently good friends are keen to share the walk with you, so a mutual arrangement to park up at either end of the chosen section of the trail could serve you well. The sketch maps show

Warning
Note that the Military Road from Heddon-on-the-Wall to Greenhead (maps 6 to 19 inclusive), used and abused by drivers as a rat-run to avoid the A69, is a potential death-trap for walkers. Please avoid using it to create any *ad hoc* circular walk.

car parking, whether formal (P in blue squares) (normally with a meter) or appropriate casual verge space (P in green squares).

Bus to Bus

The sketch maps in this guide show symbols indicating the bus stops of the 'AD122 Hadrian's Wall Bus' (out of season, service 185 plies part of the route). The regular journeys of these immensely useful buses can and should be employed. They connect the trail to the main towns and villages where accommodation is found. Once a day (end of May to end of September) the bus runs the span of the trail from Segedunum to Bowness-on-Solway (be patient with the bus on such a long route – it may well be delayed), but in the main it runs between Carlisle and Hexham via Haltwhistle. The bus enables you to enjoy a decent stretch of path without resorting to what many may consider tedious retracing of steps, or contriving a round walk, when the one thing you really want to see and stride is the frontier itself.

Check the schedule, choose your start point and board the bus; consult with the driver to further confirm pick-up points and timings to suit your pace. Be conservative in your timings. You may be a striding giant consuming two or more miles every hour, but most mortals fall short of such achievements – especially when attention is diverted to the history at your feet or the wide, bracing view or conversations with a fellow walker or local.

The use of the bus has the distinct bonus of supporting sustainable transport, bringing the personal feel-good factor into play. Despite its excellent service for tourists and walking visitors the continuation of the bus is always in the lap of the gods and under constant funding review. Consult locally for up-to-date information.

GETTING TO THE START

For the most up-to-date advice consult the current edition of the *Essential Guide* published by the Hadrian's Wall Path Trust. For those using public transport, the easiest route starts from Newcastle Central Station, which links to the Metro city train service for Wallsend, though buses may be an option.

1/32

Wallsend ⇌ Walker Riverside Park

Stride the Geordie Way by the tidal Tyne

Distance: 2.3 miles/3.7km

From the Wallsend Metro Station, wander south along Station Road to the junction with Buddle Street: ahead lies Swan Hunter Shipyard, with Segedunum Museum and its Roman fort immediately to the right.

SEGEDUNUM ROMAN FORT AND MUSEUM

The North Tyneside Council and Tyne & Wear Museum Service created the hugely impressive interpretative focus surrounding the fort, with Wall and bath-house (modelled on Cilurnum) reconstructions, a fitting tribute to the importance of this, the easternmost end of the Roman frontier. Annually it attracts 50,000 visitors, a considerable proportion being school parties from all around the country. Standing proud, among the forest of gigantic cranes in the nearby shipyard, the panoramic viewing tower evokes both the engineering heritage of the Tyne shipyards and echoes nautical architecture. In certain respects it can be said to serve a similar function to that of the London Eye.

Walkers about to embark upon the National Trail should consider investigating all parts of the museum as an essential precursor to their coast-to-coast expedition. The rather odd approach to the reception lobby was caused by the archaeology associated with the Roman track-way, which led from the eastern gate into the Barbarian territory on which the museum stands. Enter the lift to reach the high viewing gallery: a screen gives a rolling story of the site below – a most imaginative and stirring scene-setter.

Heading west, the line of the Roman Wall can be discerned to the right of a pair of tower blocks as the Fossway, the road-name a reference to the Wall's north ditch. To the right of this is the turquoise Parsons Engineering Works, and in the distance catch a glimpse of the architecturally renowned Byker Wall community housing, short of the Ouseburn. The museum's galleries are fascinating – they really do get you in the Roman frontier 'time trekker' mood. If the decision to 'do' the Wall got you here, you will need no further encouragement!

With all that has happened to the fort in recent centuries, most notably the advent of coal mining, there can be no surprise that few items of genuine fort masonry remain. However, the bath-house reconstruction should be inspected; its domed and painted interior is quite magical, conveying the sophistication of Roman culture.

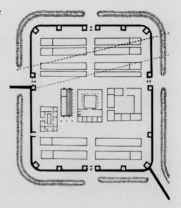

In AD122 Wall construction commenced from Hadrian's first 'grand design'. Yet only a few years elapsed before numerous adaptations were deemed essential to make the frontier more effective, and there can be little doubt Hadrian was consulted. One such change was to extend the Wall from the bridging-point of Pons Aelius to a new fort at Segedunum, as the Celts were capable of crossing the Tyne downstream of the Ouseburn. Perhaps the unrecorded fort at Gateshead was brought forward to the site of the present Newcastle keep, in the same way that Vindolanda was replaced by Vercovicium – the impressive Housesteads. Segedunum appears to mean 'strong' or 'victory' fort, clearly named to enthuse the garrison having built the Wall extension. The fort was originally garrisoned by bargemen from present-day Iraq – the skills of these early keelmen were essential in bringing garrison provisions from Arbeia. A branch Wall originally led from the south-eastern corner of the fort down to the banks of the Tyne, which was closer to the fort than today. In 1903 the few remaining Wall-stones, now set beside the cycle-path, were removed from a site within the shipyard when this was expanded to build the biggest ship ever made here, the transatlantic cruise liner 'Mauretania'.

Walkers really must visit the first true length of Roman Wall leading westwards, located within a secure enclosure outside the main fort railings, across Buddle Street. Next to the Wall stands a reconstruction showing a variety of possible finishes. The whole Wall was probably rendered and/or pointed, all with the aim of leaving the 'humbly cultured' barbarian tribes in a constant state of awe. The set of spikes or *cippi* on view are thought to have been placed in front of the Wall as an impenetrable entanglement (for reasons of public safety they are reconstructed in blunt form).

Foundations of Wall with full-height reconstruction complete with spike defences

Also visible is the sealed site of 'B' colliery shaft; the earlier 'A' pit was sunk in 1778 and lay near the west gate of the fort. Although both pits produced fine household coal, they had a terrible reputation for gas explosions. In 1835, 104 men and boys lost their lives in a single pit disaster.

The National Trail forgoes the line of the Wall as far as Heddon-on-the-Wall, preferring to follow the Tyne. The river, a tidal salt waterway, is brimming with exciting possibilities for wildlife as well as boasting an impressive history.

At present there is no marking of the line of the Wall through the city to Denton Burn – though this would be useful. But don't be put off by suburbia if you want to hold a true line, it can be done! Such a walk is better done as a personal quest or with an equally enthused friend – it's not suitable for large groups. Don't expect to find anything Roman other than the few outlines of Pons Aelius in the paving next to Newcastle's Castle Keep and in the Museum of Antiquities – located off Kings Road in the midst of the University (open all year, Monday–Saturday 10.0 –17.00, entry free, tel. 0191 2227 846).

◄◄W **WESTBOUND 1** In effect the Path begins from the back door of **Segedunum Museum**, crossing the approach road to the administrative buildings to **Swan Hunter Shipyard**. A railed path by the Wallsend Business Centre inclines up to the cycle-path (route 72 in Sustrans National Cycle Network). To the left is the Tyne Foot Tunnel some 2km away with its amazing 200ft escalator. The National Trail goes right, under the name Hadrian's Way.

The Swan Hunter company, with its distinctive red swordfish logo, is synonymous with the Tyne. There was a time when a quarter of the world's shipping was built or fitted on the Tyne. A native of Sunderland is known as a 'Makum' because many ships were built (make them: 'makum') on the Wear, then towed to be fitted on the Tyne. There are at least 20 cranes in active service even today, like giant angle-poise lamps in cheery tones of yellow, red and blue.

A notice draws attention to the large stone marking the eastern end of the National Trail opened on 23 May 2003. The modern stone, which is inscribed with all the Romans known to have been involved in the building of the Wall, can be seen more clearly from within the Segedunum enclosure. The names have been identified from Centurial Stones, which were placed by legionary gangs to record the section of Wall they constructed. These names represent a very small portion of the 15,000 or so Roman soldiers thought to have helped build the

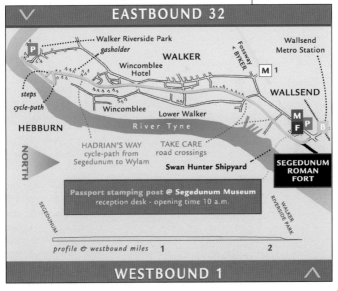

29

entire Wall. Space remains for more inscriptions to be included, should more names be discovered.

The next visible fragment of Wall emerges from the south-east corner of the fort, with an even tinier core section, down to the left, disappearing into oblivion at the base of the shabby prefabricated office building. This is the 'Walls-end'! The cycle-path now enters the Roman civilian settlement (*vicus*), where Celtic traders lived and worked in harmony with the life of the fort. They would have serviced the ancillary needs of the garrison. In light of the auxiliaries' unmarried status, services might have been of the flesh too! The red-pantile-roofed bath-house reconstruction is only accessed from within the fort site, though one gets a novel view of its construction, with its pot-vents. The original bath-house is thought to have stood upon the site of the Ship Inn, which looks diminutive next to the tall cranes. The Roman Tyne ran much closer to the fort than it does today.

On arriving at the road crossing with pedestrian traffic lights, look ahead. A bold sign confirms the end

Hadrian's Way with Branch Wall, Wallsend

of Wallsend and the beginning of the 'City of Newcastle-upon-Tyne'; close by is a metal motif of Hadrianus Augustus. Here semi-natural growth gives the trail a veil of wilderness – buddleia attracts butterflies and moths, and there is broom, elder, bramble and some Japanese knotweed, a voracious coloniser. All give small birds scope to challenge the background sounds of suburbia.

Cross another road. Notice several handy perch-seats made from rather jagged riveted girders and, widely spaced over the urban trail, the Sustrans cycle-path totem signs modelled like a shipyard chain. Whilst crossing a bridge notice the **Wincomblee Hotel**, one of a cluster of Victorian 'Gin Palaces' in this quarter of Walker. The finest, now lost, was The Neptune; four storeys high, it stood in Old Mill Road. Note the pigeon loft above the next wall; there is a cluster of them along Skinnerburn Road after Tyne Bridge. This popular working man's sport has its roots in pre-Industrial Revolution rural life. The wall directly beneath looks for all the world like Wall-stone, but of course is not, though the Ordnance Survey bench mark is authentic Victoriana and will have been etched *circa* 1861. From this point peep through the scrub growth to take the opportunity of gaining a perspective on Swan Hunter's Shipyard.

The site of Walker Station contains an impoverished soil from railway ballast, which has encouraged some unusual alkaline tolerant plants to colonise the area. The giant yellow crane of the Stena off-shore terminal looms down to the left. The verges widen, the trail runs through a green area with blue seats for repose, and a giant **gas-holder** looms shortly before the footway and cycle-path split to make their separate ways down to riverbank level. The path descends a flight of **steps** in the Walker Riverside Park. If you were thinking this trail is not a coast-to-coast adventure, as billed, then your faith will be restored now, as the banks of the river are bedecked with bladder-wrack seaweed, a sure indicator of salt water. Yes, the Tyne is tidal, and can be so all the way to Wylam. A native born along the north shore of the tidal Tyne is known as a Geordie, derived from the local diminutive for George.

➼E **EASTBOUND 32** Approaching St Anthony's Point, the trail leaves the water-front within the Walker Riverside Park – either switching steeply up steps (no sign) or taking the longer, more leisurely cycle-route – to gain the higher level of the old railway track. The walk to Segedunum couldn't be more straightforward. Keep to the cycle-path with just two road crossings – the second has pedestrian lights. Arrival at Segedunum is quite memorable, the senses a-buzz with a heady mix of shipyard cranes and Roman structures causing the eyes to whirl from one to the other with great excitement. The red pantile roof of the bath-house reconstruction (fenced off, within the fort compound) heralds arrival at the real Wallsend – a tiny section of Roman Wall can be seen emerging from the fort railings then slips down into the oblivion of the prefabricated building associated with Swan Hunter's. Just as the impressive Segedunum Museum building is passed, and opposite the Swan Hunter banner, leave the cycle-path left. A path leads down to the shipyard access road at the back of the museum (location of the passport stamping station).

Segedunum Mural

Walker Riverside Park ⇄ *Elswick*

---

*From Imperial Rome to
Imperial Britain in as many strides*

Distance: 2.9 miles/4.6km

←W WESTBOUND 2 Keep left with the riverside railing, switching orange for grey tarmac path, with a lovely open view of the great river. Growing beside the path is sea buckthorn with its distinctive orange berries in autumn. Notice the frugal remains of a ship's hull – a nervous wreck timorously hugging the sea-wall! If the freshwater Tyne is famous as the finest salmon river in England, in this tidal phase local anglers know it for its superb catches of codling and whiting. The next curve of the river makes for slacker water on the near shore. Between November and April young fishermen delight in their tight lines and screaming reels from this reach, though the billowing black smoke from their burning driftwood is a health hazard to themselves, if nothing else!

A notable exposure of mudstone topped with sandstone climbs above the path, revealing something of the carboniferous coal measure sequence. The route passes The Ropery, a 1990s terrace of bijou riverside cottages. Of rather academic interest, across the river is the Elephant-on-the-Tyne restaurant. **Friars Goose** Watersports Clubhouse is but one of several recreational facilities encountered upstream – a telling change in a once busy industrial river – and leisure speed boats are a common sight. The place-name Friars Goose comes from the old French 'le freregos', meaning sea holly, quite a rare plant which at one time must have grown along the banks of the Tyne. Spot the ornamental gulls above the archway to Trinity Courtyard before entering the plush confines of **St Peter's Marina Village** opened by Princess Diana in 1991. From the gaudy harbour offices cross the bascule counterweight-bridge and proceed via Chandlers

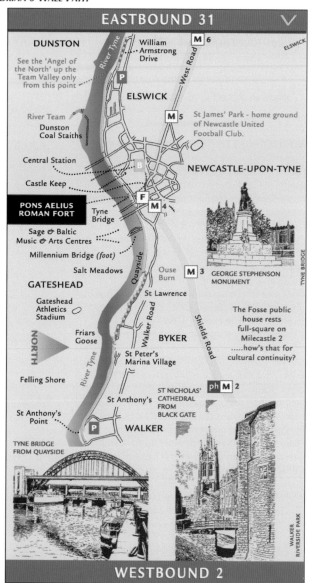

DUNSTON

See the 'Angel of the North' up the Team Valley only from this point

River Tyne

P

William Armstrong Drive

West Road

M 6

ELSWICK

ELSWICK

M 5

St James' Park – home ground of Newcastle United Football Club.

River Team

Dunston Coal Staiths

Central Station

B

NEWCASTLE-UPON-TYNE

Castle Keep

PONS AELIUS ROMAN FORT

F

M 4

Tyne Bridge

Sage & Baltic Music & Arts Centres

Millennium Bridge *(foot)*

Salt Meadows

Quayside

Ouse Burn

M 3

GEORGE STEPHENSON MONUMENT

TYNE BRIDGE

GATESHEAD

Gateshead Athletics Stadium

St Lawrence

Walker Road

Shields Road

The Fosse public house rests full-square on Milecastle 2 .....how's that for cultural continuity?

NORTH

Friars Goose

River Tyne

BYKER

St Peter's Marina Village

Felling Shore

St Anthony's

ST NICHOLAS' CATHEDRAL FROM BLACK GATE

ph **M** 2

St Anthony's Point

P

WALKER

TYNE BRIDGE FROM QUAYSIDE

WALKER RIVERSIDE PARK

Quay, with a bistro possibly the first lure to halt for casual refreshment so far.

Go right, up Glasshouse Street, turning left at the mini-roundabout between the engineering works of Bel Valves and British Engines. Now upon the footway along **St Lawrence Road**, advance past the massive white Spillers Phoenix Mill grain silo; when built in 1931, it was the largest flour mill in the world. A line of warehouses has recently been removed, thereby opening up the view of the river towards the famous sequence of Tyne bridges. Notice the old rail tracks which once brought the grain to the silos, whilst across the river are the elevators and lateral conveyors of a concrete works.

Pass Ouseburn Watersports Club, with its Admiralty pattern anchor. In crossing Ouseburn Bridge look above The Tyne Bar (noting its canny website steal!) and the overbearing Glasshouse Bridge. Then gaze in amazement at the twin-pagoda-towered brick building, all the more amazing in that it was built as a primary school! The Roman Wall crossed the Ouseburn a little upstream in the vicinity of Byker Bridge. It is a very deep cleft and must have posed quite some engineering problems; no wonder the section of Wall from Pons Aelius to Segedunum was not part of the original grand design.

Further upstream still is Jesmond Dene, 'a ribbon of green' bequeathed to the city by Lord Armstrong who died in 1900. Lord Armstrong left one of the biggest industrial legacies in British history. You may notice the statue to William Coulson above the viaduct; he was a significant benefactor to the vulnerable people and animals of Newcastle.

Keep left, holding the railing at the mouth of the **Ouse Burn**, with typically colourful harbour boats tied up alongside. Along the waterfront are the new apartments of Mariners Wharf, followed by a sequence of magnificent office buildings, architecturally projecting a modern metropolis.

The two sides of the river could not be more different. Gateshead, on the south bank, has always played second fiddle to Newcastle. However, the south bank

William Coulson Memorial backed by Ouseburn Watersports Club and the flour white Spillers Mill

now has its saving grace: the **Baltic Centre**, created from the Baltic Flour Mill silos, is now a contemporary arts centre. Even more amazing is the **Sage Music Centre**, a gleaming armadillo of a building, home of the Northern Symphonia. Combined with the not-to-be-missed Gateshead **Millennium Bridge**, these features make the blood race with excitement. Yes, you should walk over this footbridge (and back, of course, unless you fancy following the Keelman's Way upstream); its novel winking lifting action is fascinating to observe, though you'll be lucky to see it happen!

The Quayside is host to several intriguing sculptural devices, part of an extensive city-wide outdoor display. Along the Promenade are the Blacksmith's Needle and Swirle Pavilion. After the all-glass Pitcher & Piano Cafe pass Wesley Square, where John Wesley once preached. Note the backing wall etched with a map of the Tyne from Tynemouth Priory to Milecastle 42. The trail crosses the road in front of the law courts, carefully crossing the foot of Broad Chare (pronounced 'chair', this term is peculiar to Newcastle and appears to mean 'narrow way', as in the phrase 'a door ajar').

The view up the next street is dominated by the magnificent spire of All Saints Church. Pass on by the old Custom House and the Exchange Buildings, occupied by ship owners throughout the age of sail. During this era The Quayside was certainly centre-stage, for this was the second largest port in Britain. After the Slug & Lettuce pub the trail slips beneath the great green steel manacle of **Tyne Bridge**. In another setting it might be considered lumbering and unwieldy, but against the high buttressing banks it brings all into proportion. Coming to the cobbled forecourt of the Guildhall, note the two plaques by the river rails recording the visits of the Cutty Sark 'Tall Ships Race' fleet.

The red, hydraulically operated swing bridge, installed in 1876 by William Armstrong to develop his shipping and armaments factory along the Elswick riverside, rests where the Romans spanned the river with their Pons Aelius, dedicated to Emperor Hadrian. It is known that Hadrian came to these shores after inspecting the Rhine frontier; logic therefore suggests that he would have landed at the Roman port which was in the vicinity of Lort Burn. That a bridge was built with the Wall lends weight to the suggestion that there was a fort on the Gateshead side. Hadrian is thought to have influenced the design of this bridge, which may explain why his family name was ascribed to it.

NEWCASTLE – THE CULTURAL CAPITAL OF THE NORTH-EAST

Before slipping beneath the swing bridge consider a wander around the historic heart of the city. Renown for its majestic Victorian architecture, Newcastle has arguably the finest streetscapes in Britain. This guide can do scant justice to the experience, but to get you underway slip through Watergate into Sandhill, keeping left of Bessie Surtees House (a handsome 16th-century merchant's house now the north-east regional offices of English Heritage), and climb the Castle Stairs, a long flight of stone steps. These lead through the city walls at the Postern Gate, installed at the behest of Dominican monks, to the cobbled Castle Garth, with the Greek Revival-style Moot Hall to the right. Ahead stands the massive **Castle Keep**, symbolising the strength of a proud city. Visitors may enter the keep via the staircase upon the forebuilding, rather after the stamp of Dover Castle; indeed, the

Newcastle's coat of arms

Castle Keep

two castles are thought to have the same builder.

The keep stands amid the Pons Aelius site, and parts of it are laid out in the cobbles close to the base of the keep on the west side. Excavations, begun in 1978, were inevitably greatly hampered by the restricted nature of available sites; to date these have not revealed the Wall's entrance to, or exit from, the fort. Features revealed within the fort include the headquarters building, with underground strong-room to stash the cash (the Romans knew the power of money in securing allegiances); the commanding officer's buildings, with various granaries; and the Via Principalis, the main thoroughfare through the centre of the fort. The granaries are marked by three parallel lines of paving beneath the embankment arch, with a further square feature of real masonry under the arch closest to the keep. The fort was first 'spoilt' during the eighth century by conversion into a Saxon Christian cemetery in the vicinity of the keep. This was possibly associated with the monastery which gave the Newcastle its pre-Conquest name 'Monkchester'.

The importance of the Tyne as the north-country equivalent of the Thames is

Bessie Surtees House, Sandhill

Postern Gate in the City Walls from Castle Stairs

shown by the creation of the 'new castle' in 1080 by Robert Curthose, eldest son of William the Conqueror. The medieval stone castle came in the 12th century, the surviving elements being the keep from 1168, the south curtain wall, postern and north gates. medieval defences were completed during the mid-13th century by the addition of an outer north gate or barbican, now known as the Black Gate. The castle never repelled a siege and, when the town wall was completed in the mid-14th century, it stood forlorn. By the end of the 16th century only the basement of the keep and the Great Hall were still in use – as a prison and court of assize respectively. During the 17th century, houses appeared within its walls. The Civil War brought new defences – excavations in 1992 revealed a wall beneath the railway embankment arch north of the keep. By the mid-17th century shops thronged the environs of the keep, surviving until the upheavals of the 19th century, when, with ruthless efficiency, the railway embankment swept through in 1846.

Black Gate

Pass on by Black Gate, proceeding up St Nicholas Street, one's attention transfixed by St Nicholas' Cathedral. The lantern tower held high is unique in England, a 14th-century embellishment of stunning beauty. Only becoming a cathedral in 1882, the building retains the intrinsic quality of a parish church. Note the memorial bust of Thomas Bewick in Amen Corner. In 1776 Thomas moved from Eltringham near Prudhoe to a workshop located here. His wood engravings remain a vital archive, recording rural life just before the Industrial Revolution drove people from the land to labour in congested towns and cities. It is well worth visiting the museum of rural life at Bewick's birthplace in Cherryburn, near Prudhoe.

Now walk along Collingwood Street, then onto the paved isthmus to cross the traffic island with the impressive monument to George Stephenson erected in 1882. George, of 'Darlington to Stockton railway' fame, and his son, Robert, of 'Rocket' fame, lived and developed their fascination in the emergent railway revolution from works situated behind Central Station in South Street.

Begin up Westgate Road, on the line of the Roman Wall. Turn into Grainger Street, which connects Central Station with Grey's Monument. The Tyne and coal brought commerce and wealth to the city, but it was Richard Grainger's speculative building enterprise in the 1830s that brought its classical style and dignity. Booming commerce coupled with the seemingly limitless expansion of trading links with the empire (shades of Rome) brought tremendous growth – the

Thomas Bewick's memorial bust

Stephenson's Monument

city witnessed a doubling of its population during the first half of the 19th century. Grainger took advantage of the municipal wealth to put forward ideas of a coherent new Newcastle. He harnessed the architectural talent of John Dobson, and together they produced such impressive boulevards as Grainger, Grey and Clayton Streets. John Clayton of Chesters House (and, of course, Hadrian's Wall fame), the quietly spoken Town Clerk and a lawyer working in an eminent city law firm, was an influential ally. Thus, through the major building works of the Victorian Age, they created the only truly planned city centre in Britain, an ebulliently classical composition. Indeed a few years ago Grey Street was voted the most beautiful street in England by a national poll.

Dobson's final and grandest statement was the Central Station. Yet for all its merits, and for all the good it has brought the city over 150 years, there will still be those visitors with a love of history who rue the loss of the castle bailey and so much else associated pre-Industrial Newcastle – all swept aside as the railway was brought puffing and steaming into the heart of the city. A City Trail booklet can be obtained from the TIC in Princess Square. For Wall-walkers with a singular focus, a visit to Newcastle means a visit to the University of Newcastle's Museum of Antiquities. This contains the best Wall-related material found east of the North Tyne valley: there are scale models of the Wall and a *Mithreum* (Mithraic temple); bridge altars from Pons Aelius; a fine inscription *circa* AD158 recording the arrival of troops from the Rhine to reinforce the British legions. The altars, dredged from the Tyne in the 19th century, would have originally been set prominently on the Roman bridge. As Pons Aelius fort was constructed in the late second century, there is speculation regarding the

Grey's Monument

possible existence of a yet unidentified fort on the Gateshead side, coinciding with the building of the Wall. So much remains unknown about the course and nature of the Wall in this area.

Return to the foot of Castle Stairs. (In Roman times Sandhill was right on the banks of the Tyne, and plausibly a Roman harbour lay at the mouth of the Lort Burn, effectively under Tyne Bridge.) Pass under the swing bridge, and continue on by the old Fish Market (health club) and on by Lloyds Bar, built into a remnant warehouse. From medieval times onwards this area was a place of merchants. With the coming of the 'Coaly Tyne' the movement of coal along the river was handled by a rare breed of men known as keelmen. They are remembered in the lilting traditional song 'The Keel Row' (paraphrased): 'As I came through Sandgate I heard a lassie sing "Weel may the keel row The boat that my love's in".' They were hard-living men often paid in beer, and John

Hadrian's Way heading upstream from The Close

Wesley commented on their uncouthness and bad language. They became extinct with the building of the coal staithes; a large one at Wallsend is long gone, but the massive timber-framed **Dunston Coal Staithes** lingers still and comes into view on the far shore a little further along the Waterside Walkway.

From The Close, Hadrian's Way first passes beneath a spectacular sequence of bridges. First, the double-decker High Level Bridge carrying a road topped by a railway; the oldest of these bridges, it built in 1925. Then comes the Queen Elizabeth I Metro Bridge; the King Edward mainline railway bridge; and finally the sleek-lined concrete New Redheugh road bridge, built by Nuttalls. Unless you are a Geordie, defined as someone born beside the tidal Tyne, whose emotional allegiance will always be for Tyne Bridge, one and all will agree that the Gateshead Millennium Bridge is the most inspiring of the seven Tyneside spans.

Armstrong coast of arms above the Waterside Walk, Elswick

Just beyond the Copthorne Hotel, to the left of Farmers engineering consultants, an exotic, self-sown fig tree is growing from an alcove wall. The paved walkway continues beside the river railings initially near to Skinnerburn Road: spot the colourful pigeon lofts some distance along, a colourful apiarian fantasy akin to the Byker Wall housing! The trail crosses the site of the Armstrong Elswick Engineering Works, through no trace remains; in its place are river-fronting office blocks, backed at their mid-point by a flight of stairs focused on the Armstrong coat of arms. Across the water Dunston Coal Staithes dominate the scene. The riverside trail, dotted with further pieces of sculpture, eventually comes to a car park.

➩E EASTBOUND 31 Follow the paved Riverside Walkway with its occasional decking to tempt one 'onto the water'. The cycle-path ventures towards the Close, passing beneath the sequence of high-stilted bridges to merge into The Quayside. Immediately through the arch of the swing bridge one may consider diverting left via Watergate and Sandhill, then climbing the Castle Stairs to view the historic heart of the city of Newcastle from close quarters (see description above). The cycle-path leads naturally on to Wesley Square, and passes the Gateshead Millennium Bridge on a gentle curve by major office suites and Mariners Wharf apartments to the mouth of the Ouse Burn. It cuts back onto the road bridge to go past the Ouseburn Watersport Clubhouse, and along St Lawrence Road by the giant white Spillers Flour Mill silo. At the mini-roundabout turn right into Glasshouse Street, then left along Chandlers Quay to cross the bascule bridge at the entrance to St Peter's Marina. The riverside cycle-path continues by Trinity Courtyard and the Ropery. This is the point where development ceases and the tidal river takes centre stage.

Tyne Bridge from the quayside

*Gannin alang the Scotswood
Road to see the Blaydon Races*

Distance: 2.5 miles/4km

◀◀W **WESTBOUND 3** The Path continues to the very end of the pedestrian Riverside Walkway. Climb the steps beyond the British Airways building onto the latter part of William Armstrong Drive, rising to the traffic lights at the junction with Scotswood Road, at the end of the Newcastle Business Park. ▶

The surround of prestigious car dealerships, while part and parcel of the dynamic outward face of Newcastle, is, nonetheless, in stark contrast to the boarded-up housing estates that overlook the site. However, city planners have designs on this side of town: massive social upheavals are afoot, which will see the brick terraces of Elswick, Benwell and Scotswood swept away to be replaced with modern housing, causing in its train a migration to – who knows where? Cross the road at the lights, mindful that this road is destined to become a dual carriageway. Cross with caution at the foot of Whitehouse Road, signed 'Whitehouse and Condercum Industrial Estates'.

Take a moment to look back in a south-easterly direction, up the Team valley, to espy Anthony Gormley's 'Angel of the North', icon of the 1990s, just right of the 'rocket' tower block in Dunston.

One may choose to leave the Path here, diverting up this road and Atkinson Road to visit the **Benwell Nature Park** Visitor Centre and/or continue up Condercum Road to the ridge-top junction with West Road, meeting the line of Hadrian's Wall as it rises up from Pons Aelius. By following this route one visits the two surviving elements of **Condercum Roman fort**, the vallum gateway in Denhill Park and the **Temple of Antenociticus** in Broomridge Avenue. 'Condercum' meant 'wide open prospect', not exactly a reflection on the present outlook. Having broken from the trail to this extent, one will inevitably follow West Road down into Denton Dene. Alternatively walkers may venture in a more leisurely manner from the trail at the point where it reaches the footbridge over the A1 (see directions below).

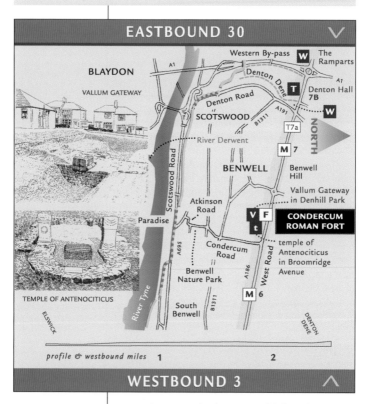

EASTBOUND 30

Western By-pass — W — The Ramparts
BLAYDON
A1
Denton Dene
VALLUM GATEWAY
T — Denton Hall 7B
A1
Denton Road
Denton Road
A191
SCOTSWOOD
B1311
W
T7a — NORTH
River Derwent
M 7
Scotswood Road
BENWELL
Benwell Hill
Vallum Gateway in Denhill Park
Atkinson Road
Paradise
V F — CONDERCUM ROMAN FORT
t
A695
Condercum Road
temple of Antenociticus in Broomridge Avenue
A186
West Road
Benwell Nature Park
M 6
TEMPLE OF ANTENOCITICUS
River Tyne
South Benwell
B1311
ELSWICK
DENTON DENE

profile & westbound miles 1   2

WESTBOUND 3

Having crossed Atkinson Road follow the footway beside **Scotswood Road**. The music-hall song 'Blaydon Races', first sung by George Ridley in 1862, refers precisely to this busy thoroughfare, recalling the lively scenes associated with the annual foot-race (earlier horse-race) which sped along the road and over

Scotswood Bridge into the town of Blaydon.

The chorus will be familiar to many:

'Oh! lads ye shud a'seen us gannin,
Passin' the folks upon the road just as they were
stannin,
Thor wis lots a lads and lasses there all wi smilin faces
Gannin alang the Scotswood Road to see the Blaydon
Races.'

The song includes the line 'Noo when we gat to Paradise
thor wes bonny gam begun'. '**Paradise**' latterly existed as
cement works set upon the site of the exotic riverside
Paradise Garden, laid out by the Hodgkins family of
Benwell House. A tiny replacement exists below the
Path and above the main road, but it has not been
properly tended.

The area from Paradise to Scotswood Bridge has
modern industrial buildings, successors to the great
Vicker's Armaments Works – hence the stationary chief-
tain tank perched at the main entrance. A drift-coal-mine
entrance is visible from the main road; the mine ran into
the bank and beneath the Whitehouse Enterprise Centre.

Follow the path inclining up right from Scotswood
Road. This wends along the course of the old Carlisle railway line (later only a mineral line) to the old Scotswood
Junction. Watch out for the fork with the Keelman's Way
bearing left over a footbridge; this leads to Scotswood
Bridge and onto the south shore of the Tyne. The old
Scotswood Station is evidenced more by the old cobbled
roadway which runs under the Path (it is worth taking a
step aside to look at the sturdy walls), a monument to
durable construction. Take the left fork, thereby avoiding
confronting the bricked-up entrance to the Scotswood
Tunnel. The cycle-path comes out at Kelly's yard on an
open area honey-combed with drift coal mines, below
Whitfield Road. The boarded-up terraces come into view,
and even a stand-alone pub has succumbed to the same
fate. Cross the **Denton Road** at the pedestrian lights and
follow the footway to where a footpath is signed left,

Dennis Frazer, Hadrian's Way Warden climbing the stairs at the old Scotswood Junction Station

There is a length of Wall foundation visible west of the massive A1/A69 roundabout junction. The pedestrian is well catered for, there being under-passes and a central footbridge enabling the walker to visit The Ramparts. This modest length of Wall gives hope for the future on our trek; the Wall next appears in more peaceful surround-ings at Heddon.

which passes the Sports Centre and weaves on to cross the A1 footbridge.

Now's your chance to break from the Trail and see the Roman sights of Denton Burn. Take the pathway lead-ing right (for anyone coming over the footbridge this would be straight on). At the first opportunity follow the pathway leading down into the Denton Burn hollow. Not a trace of water can be spotted in the dingle, but the wooded sides give an amazing sense of being in deepest countryside. The path comes up to cross a road, and advances to West Road through a strip of parkland. This leads to the library and a small section of Roman wall beside Charlie Brown's.

Go left, crossing Broadwood Road: the next length of Wall is beside Turret Road (this section includes Denton Hall turret, the only Broad Wall turret with the base of internal steps). Across the road lies the former residence of the Catholic Bishop of Newcastle. Now a nunnery, it stands serenely above the tumult of the A1. ◀

Backtrack to the east side of the roundabout via the under-passes and follow Copperas Lane (footpath), which wends close to the western by-pass but is thankfully comfortably away from the heavy traffic as it runs beside the houses. Continue alongside housing and head for the cycle-path footbridge. Cross the road – the rowdy traffic is safely underneath – just one of those trials of the trail one has to bear.

↦E EASTBOUND 30 Bear half-right, following the tarmac footway through the parkland, past the Sports Centre to Denton Road. Follow the footway to a pedestrian crossing and, opposite a boarded-up pub, bear left along an open road to Kelly's Industrial Estate. Veer right by the fencing and join the cycle-way on the old railway track-bed. Watch out, and avoid being lured onto the Keelman's Way by keeping along the progressively more open trail. Beyond the Whitehouse Enterprise Centre, a curious construction, the trail gently descends to join a footway beside the Scotswood Road. Go left, along the north side, and cross the Atkinson Road junction before crossing Scotswood Road via the traffic lights. Follow the facing road down right, by the Audi dealers, into the Newcastle Business Park. A footway leads off William Armstrong Drive to join the Riverside Walkway.

Remains of Wall at Thorntree, Denton Burn

4/29

Denton Dene ⇄ Newburn

*A railtrack trail to the
scene of the Battle of Newburn*

Distance: 1.8 miles/2.9km

◄◄W WESTBOUND 4 The tarmac footway crosses the A1 footbridge and trends left, being visually (if not audibly) screened from the terrific traffic artery. A traffic-calming island enables the suburban approach to Ottringham Close to be crossed with ease. Street names are often intriguing – this one, for instance, alludes to a village in East Yorkshire; the name means 'the ham of the people of otter-island'. Rising with the footway, rejoin the line of the rail trail, last experienced when close to the Scotswood interchange. A small chicane and the cycle-path pass the foot of Sugley Dene Nature Reserve; appropriately, the name means 'valley frequented by sparrows'.

Head on through **Lemington**, 'farmstead where brooklime grow'. Botanists will know this plant as water-pimpernel, a stream-loving member of the speedwell family – the origin of the place-name echoing its rural roots. You are now in Tyne View, with a handy row of shops. From the vicinity of the new Community Centre, over to the left, is a bee-hive-shaped **pottery kiln**.

After passing under a road bridge, the way forks; keep left. Pass the site of **Percy Pit**, now reclaimed; an incline from Walbottle Colliery once delivered coal to rail-waggon sidings here. ◄

The Path crosses the Newburn Road bridge above the Warburton's Bakery, leading on via an enormous weather-boarded building, now used for scrap cars.

The Path comes to a fork. Go left to the traffic lights beside the single-carriageway Newburn Bridge. Ignore the bridge, cross over and pass on down Water Row by

The Newburn Industrial Estate rests on the site of the huge J. Spenser & Sons Steelworks, which grew to serve the coal mining and railway industries, and is currently undergoing further changes.

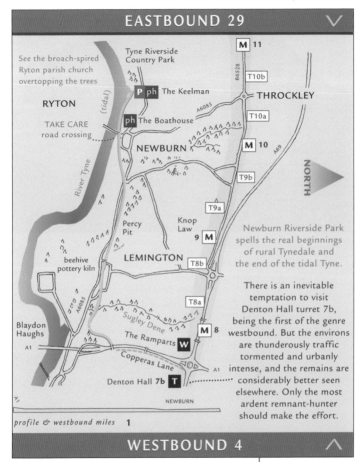

EASTBOUND 29 ∨

See the broach-spired Ryton parish church overtopping the trees

Tyne Riverside Country Park

M 11

T10b

THROCKLEY

RYTON

P ph The Keelman

(tidal)

A6085

T10a

TAKE CARE road crossing

ph The Boathouse

NEWBURN

M 10

A69

River Tyne

T9b

T9a

Percy Pit

Knop Law

9 M

Newburn Riverside Park spells the real beginnings of rural Tynedale and the end of the tidal Tyne.

LEMINGTON

T8b

beehive pottery kiln

A6085

T8a

Sugley Dene

M 8

Blaydon Haughs

The Ramparts

W

A1

Copperas Lane

Denton Hall 7b T ....

A1

NEWBURN

There is an inevitable temptation to visit Denton Hall turret 7b, being the first of the genre westbound. But the environs are thunderously traffic tormented and urbanly intense, and the remains are considerably better seen elsewhere. Only the most ardent remnant-hunter should make the effort.

profile & westbound miles   1

WESTBOUND 4 ∧

The Boathouse pub. The flood marks cut on the quoins indicate the flood of 1771 which swept away a string of bridges downstream from Bywell, including the central section of Newcastle's Tyne Bridge (on the site of the swing bridge). Although the Tyne was canalised to improve river traffic for the industrial growth of Tyneside,

51

The Keelman and Big Lamp Brewery

and in spite of the tidal nature of the river beyond this point to Wylam, this was historically the lowest fording point on the river.

In recent times dredgings were used to level the sites of the old coal-powered power stations of North and South Stella. Numerous canon balls were sieved during this process, remnants from the Battle of Newburn when a Scottish army, led by General Lesley, overwhelmed Charles I's English army positioned on the Ryton bank on 28th August 1640.

The tall, broach-spired Ryton church appears above the woodland, on the far side of a stretch of river that, at high tide, looks more like a lake. Pass the Tyne Rowing Club, with its head of Old Father Tyne sporting a twisted beard capped with a basket of coal. The cycle-path arrives at the **Tyne Riverside Country Park** with its visitor centre; behind this is the Big Lamp Brewery and **The Keelman** bar and restaurant. ◄

The house ale can be bought in two-pint jugs for the price of one and a half pints – bad news for walkers trying to cultivate a good walking pace!

The building was originally a pumping house for the local Isabella Colliery. The coal was transformed into coke, the sulphur being removed in ovens, thus enabling it to be used at Spenser's Steelworks and the Solway Hematite Iron Company.

Robert Stephenson lived for a time in Newburn, and first experimented with his famous 'Rocket' locomotive on the Wylam Waggonway. Laid in 1813, the track later saw the Wylam Dilly and Puffing Billy hauling coal waggons. The waggonway was essential, as the river at the time was too shallow for keeled boats. An interesting fact is that the standard gauge of these railways precisely matches the width of a Roman cart, 4' 8½" – can this possibly be a coincidence?

➠**E EASTBOUND 29** Leave the slipway, keeping on the riverbank path to the Tyne Rowing Clubhouse and The Boathouse pub in Water Row. Once a signal box stood next to a level-crossing at Newburn Bridge (see the photograph on the wall in the pub). Cross straight over at the traffic lights, veering immediately left onto the track-bed trail. This is the course of the first Carlisle to Newcastle Railway, which was later used as a mineral line when the new main line forged a route on the south bank of the Tyne. Keep to the hard tarmac cycle-path; it ends at an estate road crossing in Bell's Close. The route then rises in a landscaped open space and crosses the footbridge spanning the Western Bypass.

5/28

Newburn ⇄ Heddon-on-the-Wall

Head to Heddon – meet the wall head on

Distance: 3.8 miles/6km

◄W WESTBOUND 5 The Tyne Riverside Country Park represents the beginnings of the country trail, extending from this site at Newburn as a tendril with the Wylam Waggonway the six miles to Low Prudhoe. William Hedley's famous 'Puffing Billy' ran this way, the first smooth-tracked, smooth-wheeled locomotive.

Natural river-bank erosion adjacent to the path approaching the Wylam Waggonway

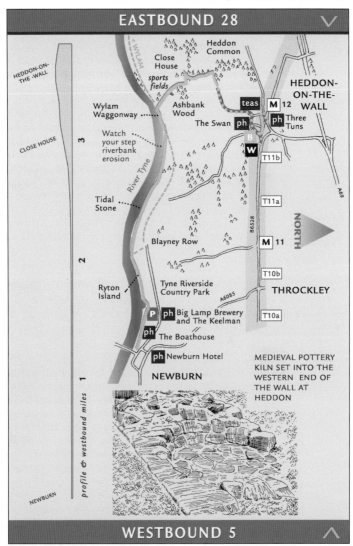

EASTBOUND 28 ⌄

HEDDON-ON-THE -WALL

CLOSE HOUSE

Heddon Common

Close House

sports fields

< WYLAM

Wylam Waggonway ·······

Ashbank Wood

teas

M 12

HEDDON-ON-THE-WALL

The Swan **ph**

ph Three Tuns

B

W

T11b

Watch your step riverbank erosion ·······

River Tyne

Tidal Stone ·······

T11a

B6528

A69

NORTH ▶

Blayney Row

M 11

T10b

Ryton Island

Tyne Riverside Country Park

A6085

THROCKLEY

T10a

P **ph** Big Lamp Brewery and The Keelman

ph The Boathouse

ph Newburn Hotel

NEWBURN

MEDIEVAL POTTERY KILN SET INTO THE WESTERN END OF THE WALL AT HEDDON

profile ⮂ westbound miles

1   2   3

NEWBURN

WESTBOUND 5 ⌃

Steam on upstream beside the river, where salmon can be seen leaping. Pass an area known as **Ryton Island**, so called from the time when it was indeed an island and was quirkily claimed as part of County Durham. Much as the name 'Newburn' reflects the changing course of the feeder stream, the Tyne has been drawn into one tidal waterway, and at high-tide this gives the impression of a great lake. As the path splits notice the wooden stump associated with an old ferry landing; the boatman's house remains on the far bank. A kissing-gate leads on beneath the hedge-line: note the **Tidal Stone**, marking the limit of salt water; the river level is, nonetheless, affected almost up to Prudhoe. Continue along the riverbank. Further along there is considerable evidence of bank erosion, at this point caused by the river, not by walkers. Go through the kissing-gate onto the Wylam Waggonway, a popular recreational bridleway. Go left some 160 yards to find a kissing-gate, right.

You may like to follow the Waggonway for a further mile to visit the little cottage where George Stephenson was born. The curious name Wylam means 'village with a salmon trick or trap'.

Traverse the golf course fairway, watchful for the movement of golfers. A green causeway leads on by a pond, with an open cricket ground and pavilion over to the left. Slip through the cricketers' car park, and follow the succeeding lane uphill. The track curves left passing glass-houses and a walled garden to a gate barrier at the back of Close House, currently the property of the University of Newcastle. It was built in 1779 in the classical style for the Berwicke family, successful Merchant Adventurers in Newcastle.

Switch acutely right, up the holly-lined lane signed for Heddon. The partially cobbled track runs through woodland to a gate by a cottage, rising with rank holly growth in flanking hedge. The track encounters another woodland beneath a pylon line; at this point bear right, passing West Acre and another power-line. The near pylon is awkwardly perched above a deep sandstone quarry. Pass a cluster of well-favoured houses enjoying a fine view over the Tyne valley towards Newburn and Benwell Hill, site of Condercum Roman fort. The bungalow, South Lodge, shows an exaggerated Mediterranean influence.

Rising by Heddon Banks, venture into an area of estate roads with such names as Trajan Walk and Centurion Way, giving clues to the proximity of matters Roman. There is a small shopping area, left, including the Dingle Dell tea-room, renown for its bespoke packed lunches using local produce. The Trail turns right into Towne Gate. Opposite the **Swan** Hotel one may take the path to St Andrew's Church, the prominent hilltop situation correctly suggesting a pious place of some antiquity. ▶

The Trail follows on along Towne Gate, passing a bus shelter (regular buses service) and timber-built Women's Institute.

The Trail is directed left into Chare Bank, but do not hasten on too quickly; by pacing a further 100 yards one may enter, via a kissing-gate on the right, an enclosure containing… Hadrian's Wall. 'Heddon' means 'the heath-covered hilltop settlement on Hadrian's Wall', and here it is. How it survived goodness only knows. Wall walkers, who are by now weary of the meagre fare thus far served up in the name of Emperor Hadrian, can gaze upon a real length of consolidated masonry, with much Roman tooling evident. The near end shows the base of a post-Roman, probably medieval, pottery kiln, apparently built into what will have been a much taller standing wall, probably with other timber dwellings attached too. What was to become the village of Heddon will have hugged the Wall for many centuries. With the gorse bank of Great Hill as a backdrop and some evidence of the north ditch before us, you can gaze upon a credible length of Wall showing an original kink, miraculously ignored by the Military Road engineers. It stretches for 110yds/125m and rises to a maximum of six courses.

A church appears to have stood on this site since about AD650 – little wonder, then, that the chancel is laden with fine courses of Wall-stone. A rookery in the adjacent beech trees gives a raucous country greeting.

Grooved tooling on Wall at Heddon

The monument is beautifully tended by English Heritage, and while we perforce view this portion in glorious isolation, it is, for the very first time, possible to spin the imagination back across the gulf of 18 centuries to when the Wall was a continuous high stone divide, the northern limit of Roman authority in Britannia. Even cattle grazing in the adjoining ridge-and-furrow pasture symbolise the long continuity of civilian life during intervening centuries.

Pottery Kiln at Heddon

Now, convinced you are back on course with the Roman military frontier, backtrack to Chare Bank, a minor bridle-lane leading by Amos Brothers 'Roman Wall Forge' down to the Village Hall. Turn right, and carefully cross the busy road to the junction by **Three Tuns** public house, turning left onto the footway beside the Military Road. One can sense at last that the long westward march with the Wall is beginning.

↠E EASTBOUND 28 Cross over the road at the Three Tuns following the village road to the right of the memorial gardens. In front of the village hall go past the white barrier into Chare Bank; this pathway emerges into Towne Gate. Turn left to visit the English Heritage Wall site a matter of 100 yards further on; enter via a kissing gate. Backtrack along Towne Gate, passing The Swan Hotel, turning left down the road by Heddon Banks. The road becomes a track by West Acre.

Slipping under power-lines the lane bears left from the woodland of Heddon Common, down by a cottage, via a gate into a wooded, partially cobble lane lined with holly, then down to the rear of Close House. Go left by the white barrier, passing the walled garden and glass-houses; the lane curves right, down to a car park for the sports field (in summer this means cricket). Keep forward, along the green causeway with a pond to the left, and pass through a golf course to join the Wylam Waggonway at a kissing-gate. Go left and, after some 160 yards go right through a kissing-gate to follow the path hugging the banks of the Tyne to arrive at the slipway at the Tyne Riverside Country Park. Close by, the visitor centre is certainly worth inspecting. The Keelman Restaurant and Big Lamp Brewery located behind the centre will have their own appeal!

The wall at Heddon

6/27

Heddon-on-the-Wall ⇄ Harlow Hill

The Roman frontier stretches out,
mile after a Roman country mile

Distance: 4 miles/6.4km

←W **WESTBOUND 6** Setting out upon the footway from the Three Tuns with the north ditch to the right over the wall, the Military Road stretches like a gun barrel into the distance. The A69 intervenes to steal its continuity, causing the B6318 to veer sharp right. At the flyover there is no footway; cross the road to step over the crash barrier at the end. Follow the grass verge down the incline to the resumption of the Military Road. ◀

This is the course of Wade's Military Road constructed in 1747 after the Jacobite Rebellion. It ran from the heart of Newcastle to Sewingshields. With robust symbolism the contracted engineers requisitioned the Wall as hardcore.

Today the road is terrorised by heavy lorries and plagued with speeding cars, as drivers love the roller coaster ride as a rat-run variant to the A69. The B6318 dominates the Roman frontier from here to the onset of the Whin Sill escarpment. As a means of fossilising the foundations of Hadrian's Wall it may seem a brutal preservation. However, in years yet to come, the masonry entombed by tarmac may prove a fertile *terra nova* for research.

Cross a stile, step down into the pasture and follow the roadside hedge. Cast off, as well you can, the trappings of modern 'civilisation', the noisy A69 and the pylon line. Study the few loose vestige courses of Wall-stone occasionally evident at the foot of the hedge close right (notice that the vallum has influenced the field boundaries). Beyond an intermediate gate and on reaching the field-corner copse, angle half-left to a kissing-gate, cross the minor road to the right of the farm buildings at Rudchester.

The Military Road sliced through the middle of the Roman fort of Vindovala. The fourth fort, it covered an area of four and a half acres and lies seven Roman miles

16 M
Harlow Hill
P

< HORSLEY

T15b

Old church incorporated into farmyard - a
sad secular demise of a lovely building;
admire the little round turret tower
beside the porch - it deserved a better fate.

HARLOW HILL

ALBEMARLE BARRACKS >

4

GB garage:
walkers will have GruB
in their minds, hence the
Robin Hood Inn can't
come soon enough, just
two Milecastles away!

T15a

Three ages of military way focus
upon this one spot, modern NATO,
the post-Jacobite highway and
Roman Frontier Wall, which had
its (now lost) service way too.

M 15

TAKE CARE
crossing road

T14b

Iron Sign - a little bit of Dallas on the Wall,
cattle-ranch fencing and 'South Fork'
architecture. Though it has to be said the
red pantile roof and white-washed walls
hint to a Roman domestic villa.

3

*grand
westward view*
Eppies Hill
High Seat

T14a

< OVINGTON   WHITCHESTER >

Iron Sign Country House Restaurant

M 14

March Burn

residual drystone
Wall in hedge bank

ridge & furrow

2

< HORSLEY
Rudchester
House

F   **VINDOVALA ROMAN FORT**

PONTELAND >

< CORBRIDGE

T13a

The farm-buildings at Rudchester would
make a superb Roman-theme
visitor centre - in years to come,
well, it just may happen!

EPPIES HILL

M 13

*path follows
wide verge*

HEDDON
MILL >

NORTH

*cross road on
flyover bridge*

step over barrier

1

A69

footway

RUDCHESTER

The Swan

ph   ph   Three
Tuns

M 12

NEWCASTLE >

Residual drystone Wall in base of
hedge surviving from the brutally
destructive construction of the
Military Road in the mid-1750s

**HEDDON-ON-
THE-WALL**

A69 fumes and noise pollution...
......the exhaust pipe of the city!

profile ⟳ westbound miles

Evidence of the Wall in the roadside bank approaching Rudchester

west of Condercum. The basic outline of the fort can be seen both to the north, defined by the wooden paddock fencing, and to the south, by the farm buildings. The sturdy sandstone barn would appear to contain a few Roman stones, particularly in its lower courses. The Wall's first serious commentator, J.Collingwood Bruce, author of the *Handbook to the Roman Wall*, noted in 1860 that there were fragments of a Roman gravestone on an inside wall, inscribed with the letters: AVR, RIN, XIT, NIS.

MITHRAIC TEMPLE

A Mithraic temple has been excavated to the south-east of the fort. There were several temples to the god Mithras along the wall, the focus of a religious cult whose practices can be very loosely paralleled with present-day masonic ritual. Derived from ancient Persia, the cult was preferred by officers, notably legionaries, though evidently auxiliaries drew inspiration from it too. It was exclusively masculine in observance, associated with mysterious acts linked to the sacrificial slaying of bulls in a cave, and focused on the eternal battle between light (good) and dark (evil). In its heyday it rivalled Christianity in popularity. Ironically the present farm-name 'Rudchester' inverts the Roman chauvinism, for it translates as 'the former Roman fort now belonging to Rudda', a Scandinavian feminine name.

Head straight on, and at the fence bear right along-side to a stile in the corner. Notice a few Wall stones again in the hedge foot and the invasive growth of elder dominating the hawthorn. Cross the stile, descend the pasture with well-marked ridge-and-furrow ploughing evident. The ridges run in two directions with broader, possibly later, curved ridges close to hand; these may be indicative of ox-ploughing. There is evidence of Wall-stone in the bank (right), most notable in the walling leading into the road bridge spanning March Burn. Cross the stile and succeeding footbridge. March Burn means 'the boundary stream' – notice the well house. Note that the flag-steps (right) have no practical purpose for Path users.

Continue along the edge of the arable field to a paling fence. The prominent white house ahead is the former **Iron Sign Farm**. The Path follows the fencing on an elaborate square perambulation to reach the minor road; go right for the road junction at Two Hoots. Go left; a broad pathway draws into a passage by boarding, shielding a massive lawned garden. Pass through a hand-gate at the brow of **Eppies Hill** to emerge on the field edge with a lovely open prospect ahead. ▶

The Path descends to cross the busy road: pay great attention, as cars come at a ferocious pace. Steps descend from a platform into the north ditch; a fenced passage ensues, currently on a robust hardcore base. At the corner go via a hand-gate then cross a plank-bridge over the ditch; this wild section, shaded by gorse and thorn scrub, is the north ditch. Stone flags line the shallower portion of the north ditch leading to the peaked corner. Go through the hand-gate onto the minor road to Whitchester.

Take the corresponding hand-gate and follow the edge of the field to another hand-gate at the broad road entrance to the **Albemarle Barracks** – a modern military way diverging from the Roman and post-Jacobite military ways. Continue forward via a hand-gate with a fence to the right once more. This leads up the hill, and a big garage sign heralds arrival at the hamlet of **Harlow Hill**. The barn and farmhouse before the old church are entirely constructed with Wall-stone. The small church

Notice the steam, half-left, emitting from Prudhoe Paper Pulp works, while a similar cloud may also be spotted further ahead, this being the distant plume of Eggers cardboard mill at Hexham. Together these enterprises have caused the RAF to nickname Tynedale the 'Blue Valley'.

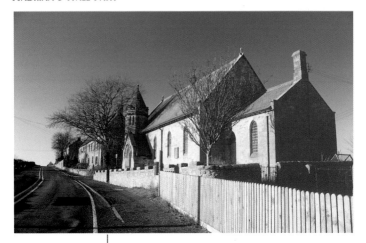

Converted church at Harlow Hill has a delightfully proportioned round tower beside the porch, though sadly the building has been deconsecrated, with a crude sliding door set into the north wall; its services are prosaically agricultural. The wooded top of Heddon-on-the-Wall, three miles distant, forms the eastern horizon.

➡E EASTBOUND 27 The Path hugs the B6318 on one side or the other to Eppies Hill, with one exposed road crossing to heed. A roadside pathway leads to a minor road junction; go right, passing the entrance to the former Iron Sign Farm, now a country house restaurant. Find a passage to the left which accommodates the Path around a large square paddock and come back to the roadside hedge line once more, then continue east to a footbridge over March Burn. Keep up beside the hedge to a stile, then go right skirting the shallow banks of Vindovala Roman fort and the farm buildings. (In an ideal world this would be an exhibition fort for visitors to the eastern country end of the Wall system.) Cross the minor road by facing kissing-gates angling half-left to continue beside the roadside hedge down to a stile adjacent to the embankment of the A69. Follow the verge of the re-aligned B6318, step over the barriers at the top and cross the road in the middle of the flyover following the footway up to Heddon.

Harlow Hill ⇄ Woodhouses Road-End

*The Wall is whittle'd down to nought;
brisk pacing towards the second stamping post*

Distance: 2.25 miles/3.5km

◄►W WESTBOUND 7 At the top of the hill, after the farm, cross a wall-stile on the right and descend the conifer enclosure to a wall-squeeze to enter a fenced passage beside the road. ►

Pass along a gravel path beside the reservoir. Traverse a linking channel bridge to run alongside the road-barrier, and cross the road junction via corresponding hand-gates. From the next hand-gate a flagged path rises, then passes a stone bench some 100 yards along; continue within what is left of the north ditch. Take the hand-gate at the top of the rise; the Path now follows the berm (top edge) of the north ditch, after 30 yards passing a stone Path marker. At the next hedge a hand-gate with a fence excludes the path from the north ditch and open pasture right.

A new hedge has been planted alongside the road, a grant-aided farmland improvement scheme and an asset to the Path too. Go through another hand-gate and across

The **Whittledene Reservoirs** are set on various stepped levels, the adjacent waters popular with vagrant water-fowl. Watch out for young or female smew, a small sea duck with a red head; grebes, Great and Little, both nest here. Anglers, too, are given licence to enjoy these shining levels. Whittle means 'the hill with the large expanse of dry land' – but the dams have sorted that out good and proper!

Robin Hood Inn

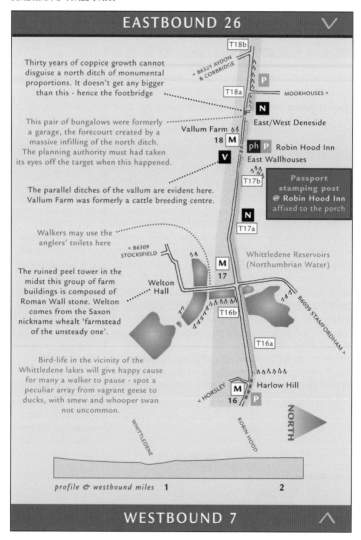

EASTBOUND 26

T18b

< B6321 AYDON & CORBRIDGE

P

T18a

MOORHOUSES >

N

Thirty years of coppice growth cannot disguise a north ditch of monumental proportions. It doesn't get any bigger than this - hence the footbridge

East/West Deneside

Vallum Farm

18 M

This pair of bungalows were formerly a garage, the forecourt created by a massive infilling of the north ditch. The planning authority must had taken its eyes off the target when this happened.

V

ph P Robin Hood Inn

East Wallhouses

T17b

Passport stamping post @ Robin Hood Inn affixed to the porch

The parallel ditches of the vallum are evident here. Vallum Farm was formerly a cattle breeding centre.

N

T17a

Walkers may use the anglers' toilets here

< B6309 STOCKSFIELD

Whittledene Reservoirs (Northumbrian Water)

M

17

Welton Hall

The ruined peel tower in the midst this group of farm buildings is composed of Roman Wall stone. Welton comes from the Saxon nickname whealt 'farmstead of the unsteady one'.

B6009 STAMFORDHAM >

T16b

T16a

Bird-life in the vicinity of the Whittledene lakes will give happy cause for many a walker to pause - spot a peculiar array from vagrant geese to ducks, with smew and whooper swan not uncommon.

< HORSLEY

M

16

Harlow Hill

P

NORTH

WHITTLEDENE

ROBIN HOOD

profile & westbound miles **1**   **2**

WESTBOUND 7

North ditch heading west to the Robin Hood Inn

a farm track with open access to the Military Road, left; continue over a plank spanning a small dyke. At the end of the next field climb steps, and go sharp left then right to cross the forecourt of the Robin Hood Inn. This busy road-house has cultivated trade to such an extent that walkers, in high season, can have a long wait for attention; food is served all day at weekends. Pass on along the road verge to a hand-gate, then walk alongside some free-range hens and via two kissing-gates to enter the north ditch flanked by gorse. A hand-gate leads onto a track at Deneside, a former roadside garage, hence the loss of the north ditch. One wonders how the planners were so duped to allow the archaeology to be so wantonly foregone.

The Path follows the road verge with a massive north ditch. **Vallum Farm** on the south side is well named, the vallum being very evident especially to the west; along with ridge and furrow it runs parallel to the road. The Path finds sanctuary from the highway via a handsome footbridge spanning the north ditch. The landscaping coppice within the ditch is of some 35 years' growth; before that time the ditch was open. The Path runs on, with a fence to the right against arable land, to a wall-stile at Woodhouses road end. This is a useful space for casual car parking.

↦E EASTBOUND 26 From the Woodhouses road end (with the Hadrian's Wall Pet Hotel sign prominent) cross the wall-stile. Proceed with a fence left, the wooded north ditch right and Harlow Hill in view ahead. Cross the footbridge erected to take the trail over the massive north ditch. Follow the road verge by Deneside, dipping back into the north ditch left at steps. Two kissing-gates and a hand-gate lead to the car park at the Robin Hood. Continue along the verge, and descend steps left into the north ditch. The Path, fenced from the arable land, runs within the remains of the north ditch alongside the main road. Latterly flagged, it crosses the B-road at its junction with the Military Road via facing hand-gates. Now with road barriers right, cross the reservoir bridge to a hand-gate, tucked under the dam banking on a gravel path. The Path rises via a wall-gap and a rough bank containing conifers to a wall-stile at Harlow Hill.

Welton Hall Farm

8/25

Woodhouses
Road-End ⇄ Halton Shields

In rapport with the Wall
through an arable landscape

Distance: 1.9 miles/3.3km

◄◄W WESTBOUND 8 From the wall-stile at Woodhouses road-end, cross road and go over the wall-stile opposite, with a fence to the right and the north ditch crowded with larch trees. After a stile the larches dwindle until the path is ushered left at a low wall through the shallow north ditch to a ladder-stile onto the main road. ▶

Follow the verge in front of **Wallhouses Farm**, and note the concreted cattle sorting pen in the north ditch.

The speed of traffic is a great cause for concern here. (It would be wonderful if a slither of land could be set

Opposite, a sign directs south at a junction to the Fi Fie Fo Fum Art Gallery: this contemporary country-life centre and art gallery at Newton promotes rising local artists who specialise in interpreting the Northumberland landscape.

Field edge path
near the site of
Milecastle 19

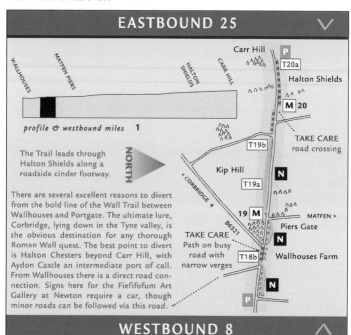

EASTBOUND 25 ⌄

WALLHOUSES · MATFEN PIERS · HALTON SHIELDS · CARR HILL

Carr Hill

P

T20a

Halton Shields

M 20

profile & westbound miles 1

TAKE CARE
road crossing

NORTH

The Trail leads through
Halton Shields along a
roadside cinder footway.

T19b

Kip Hill

< CORBRIDGE 4

T19a

N

There are several excellent reasons to divert
from the bold line of the Wall Trail between
Wallhouses and Portgate. The ultimate lure,
Corbridge, lying down in the Tyne valley, is
the obvious destination for any thorough
Roman Wall quest. The best point to divert
is Halton Chesters beyond Carr Hill, with
Aydon Castle an intermediate port of call.
From Wallhouses there is a direct road con-
nection. Signs here for the Fiefifofum Art
Gallery at Newton require a car, though
minor roads can be followed via this road.

19 M

B6321

MATFEN >

Piers Gate

TAKE CARE
Path on busy
road with
narrow verges

T18b

N

Wallhouses Farm

N

P

WESTBOUND 8 ⌃

aside for the safe progress of Hadrian's Wall Path walkers.) A walled field, access right, comes to the walker's
aid as the Path re-enters the security of the wooded north
ditch enclosure: note the curved ox-ploughing ridge-and-
furrow in the adjacent pasture angling away to the north.
Cross the next stile at the **Piers Gate** delta road junction.
The ball-topped stone pillars, right, herald the approach
road to Matfen Hall, now a country house hotel. The two
Saxon village names on the road sign are intriguing:
Matfen means 'Matta's peat marsh', whilst Ingoe means
'Inga's hill'.

The Path goes left. Cautiously cross the Military Road
to the hand-gate beside the Tynedale District 'Hadrian's
Wall Country' sign. You have just left Castle Morpeth
District. The Trail runs on beside the roadside hedge,

fenced from the field some four feet below road level – the difference being the Wall foundations. Spot the occasional residual Wall-stones in the base of the bank – at one point there is a veritable feast of dry-stone walling from Hadrian's age. At a minor road junction the Path crosses a stepped wall-stile and, from a short flagged path, ventures onto a cinder-based surface along the broad verge beside main road. Note the steam rising from Eggers, a cardboard pulp-mill at Hexham, half left.

The Trail switches across the main road to the northern verge just short of the **Halton Shields** sign. At the western end of the little community, after the old primary school, is a telephone kiosk and post box. ▶

The roadside path comes to a conclusion at a casual lay-by opposite the farm entrance to **Carr Hill**, where it switches sides. ▶

The hamlet name harbours more than you might suspect – Shields means 'a cluster of shepherd's summer dwellings', while Halton come from the Saxon 'haw-hyll', meaning 'look-out hill'.

The name Carr is curious – normally associated with boggy hollows, it is here found upon a hilltop. It may be a contraction of the Celtic 'carreg', meaning 'the rocks', to match Carraw Farm beyond Brocolitia Roman fort.

⮕E EASTBOUND 25 Cross to the lay-by and follow the cinder path along the northern verge of the Military Road, passing the hamlet of Halton Shields. At the site of Milecastle 20 cross over, continue to the minor road junction, cross the wall-stile opposite and embark on the fenced passage with arable land set below the roadside hedge bank. A hand-gate brings the Path to a road crossing at Piers Gate, a wall-stile gives entry to the confines of the north ditch, and a further stile brings the Path back onto the Military Road for a couple of hundred yards, passing Wallhouses Farm. Dip left, back into the north ditch enclosure, within a larch copse to a wall-stile and the Woodhouses road-end.

9/24

Halton Shields ⇄ *The Portgate*

Downhill to Corstopitum

Distance: 1.4 miles/2.2km

◀◀W **WESTBOUND 9** Cross the Military Road at the lay-by opposite the access to Carr Hill Farm. The Path now follows the grass verge on the south side of the road to a wall-stile. From here, the vallum takes centre stage. After 40 yards a recessed gate causes the Path to slip over

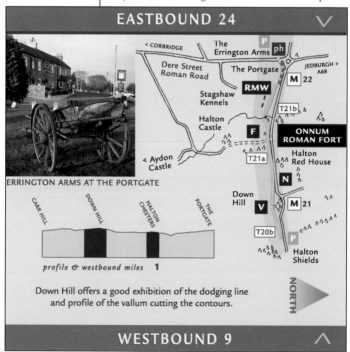

EASTBOUND 24

ERRINGTON ARMS AT THE PORTGATE

Down Hill offers a good exhibition of the dodging line and profile of the vallum cutting the contours.

WESTBOUND 9

facing wall-stiles, with fence left, until a stile heralds its release into open pasture on **Down Hill**. There has been considerable surface quarrying, left unkempt, the greater quarry being on the west side of the plantation. The Path takes the natural course, sweeping over the brow and passing a stone trail-marker set beside a particularly stunning section of vallum bank and ditch. The route has comparatively few close encounters with the vallum, so savour this. ▶

There are also 'crossings' in this section – gaps where the ditch was in-filled during a later Roman period when the tight rein of the military zone was relaxed; they served to funnel all movement through the wall to the milecastle gates and, in this locality, the great Dere Street frontier control at up-coming Portgate.

Head downhill, crossing an open track, and aim half-right to the corner of the field by the road, then cross a wall-stile. The Path, with wall right and light fence left, is four feet below the level of the road. A field access gate causes a twin-stile break in the fence passage just before **Halton Red House**, a handsome farmhouse set on the north side of the main road. Cross the wall-stile at the next wall junction and keep beside the roadside wall via

The vallum on Down Hill

Notice the angular engineered turns of the vallum just prior to the crest of Down Hill, a characteristic throughout its course. Just as the Romans liked straight roads, so they liked sharp turns rather than wavy lines.

a fenced passage. In this area ridge-and-furrow abounds, the curved line betraying ox-ploughing.

A stile gains entry into what would appear to be parkland. An open drive leads left, down to **Halton Castle**, from the stone gateway off the Military Road. At your feet, the shallow undulations hint at unidentified underlying features of Onnum Roman fort. Known as Halton Chesters, this cavalry fort, 4.3 acres in extent, lies seven miles west of Vindovala. That it was built by the VI Legion Augusta is verified by the stone plaque inserted above the west gate. A further inscription, referring to subsequent work by the II Legion during the reign of Antoninus Pius now resides in the Museum of Antiquities in Newcastle. The name Onnum is Celtic for 'water', and may simply refer to a sure supply of water, in contrast to Aesica (Great Chesters) with its seven-mile-long feeder aqueduct. One unusual feature was the bath-house which lay within the vallum, close to the fort.

GOOD CAUSE TO CORSTOPITUM

A National Trail, within bounds of a World Heritage Site, merits the occasional diversion from the route, so why not venture down the open drive to view

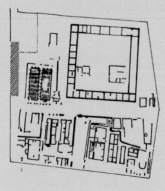

Corstopitum site plan

Halton Castle, and/or as a greater diversion visit the English Heritage sites of **Aydon Castle** and **Corstopitum** at Corbridge, bringing ever richer rewards to the heritage experience. Indeed, Corbridge is a good place to enjoy a half-day break away from a heavy walking schedule. Halton Castle is not open to the public, but from the passing by-road one can get a good sight of this sturdy, high-chimneyed house set into a castellated peel tower: defensive medieval domesticity. A winding country lane leads on to Aydon Castle, perched upon a blunt bluff,

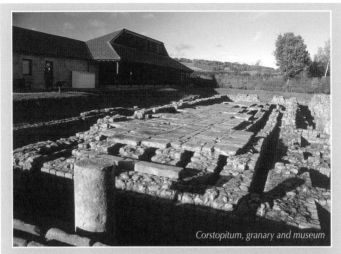

Corstopitum, granary and museum

embraced by beechwood, above a tight bend in Cor Burn. Both castles have former connections with the Matfen Estate.

Aydon's situation is stunning, and is often cited as the finest defended medieval manor house in England. In years gone by it has been a popular film set for such films as 'Ivanhoe'. The main body of the property is unadulterated 14th-century work, built by a Suffolk merchant who had cause to rue his adventure north. The Middle Ages in the Middle Marches were no place for peaceable people, when Scottish raids and local reiving made farming life precarious and costly.

A footpath leads on to Aydon Road, entering Corbridge via Princes Street. At the centre is St Andrew's Church, which has a complete Roman arch, from the Roman town, incorporated into the original construction. On the west side of the church are the 14th-century King's Ovens – the townsfolk had to bake bread communally as dough was taxed. Dere Street is erroneously named Watling Street in the town. The town today attracts visitors in a stylish way reminiscent of Chipping

Corbridge Lion

75

Corbridge – Corstopitum

Campden in the Cotswolds or Ludlow in Shropshire. It takes its role seriously – it is a town of substance. However, Corbridge has something unique to offer – Corstopitum.

Though apparently well removed from the town, the Roman Corstopitum, extending some 24 hectares, almost butts up to the modern settlement. It is worth noting that only some 7 percent of the Roman settlement has been revealed. Adjacent, though unseen, a massive Roman bridge, built upon 10 piers, spanned the Tyne; the river has drifted south from its Roman course. In the north bank, footings of a triumphal gateway have been found. This originally stood over Dere Street, the road from York (Eboricum), and proclaimed southern entry into this evidently important military town. Pre-dating Hadrian's Wall, Corstopitum is situated at the eastern end of the Stanegate, the military way from Carlisle.

Using the Hadrian's Wall Bus one can venture to Hexham, rejoining the Wall walk at Wall village; alternatively, one can go by Milkwell Lane, footpath and lane via Stagshaw Kennels to regain Halton Chesters on a variant return, thus keeping faith with every stride of the trail.

Lane from Aydon Castle

A ladder-stile exits in the fort enclosure at Onnum. The Path, running alongside arable land, is guided away from the road by a small triangular plantation. Proceeding down to a ladder-stile, cross a fence then flagged footbridge over a cattle-puddled brook. The Path veers half-right up pasture coming alongside the road-fence by a stone trail-marker. Cross a stile beside a new cattle-holding pen, then, 300 yards up, a ladder-stile pitches the Path over the wall and onto the broad verge leading up to the Portgate cross-roads by Fawdrington's garage. Cross the A68 to the left of the **Errington Arms**, perhaps admiring the light farm carts on display. Though the carts are painted, the decaying process is little halted; what a contrast with the '4x4s' on show across the way!

PORTGATE

The A68 follows the line of a major prehistoric trade route, far older than the Roman Dere Street. This meeting place became known in Saxon times as 'the port-gate' because of its regional importance as a place of barter. It was later the site of Stagshaw Fair, the largest open-air livestock market in England. Where the roundabout now stands the Romans built a great fortified gate; it was out of kilter with the tidy order of Wall structures specifically to marshal this convergence of age-old roads.

Writing in 1732, John Horsley stated that the Roman fortified gate in the Wall was still *in situ*. To what forlorn height it had languished by that time we have no record, but it is yet another stark reminder of the cruel loss of an important component of the Wall's structure. It was located in the space between the inn and traffic roundabout. This was a significant Roman control on what in later years was termed Dere Street.

This arterial military road stemmed from York, the northern command base for the Roman province. It strode north, entering the frontier zone at Corbridge, some three miles south of this spot. Advancing from here it proceeded northbound for Risingham, High Rochester and Chew Green, where it then crossed the Cheviot Hills bound for Melrose. Anyone who has admired the famous 'Scott's View' will know of the Eildon hills above that town, reflected in the Roman name for the fort – Trimontium ('place at the three hills').

➼E EASTBOUND 24 The Path crosses the A68 from the car park of the Errington Arms. Follow a footway on the tapering verge from the roundabout, and step down a ladder-stile into the pasture on the right. Proceed via a fence-stile to a flag-footbridge and ladder-stile; ascend with the small plantation on the left. Go along the field edge to a ladder-stile into the Halton Chesters enclosure. Pass the stone entrance to Halton Castle drive, proceed to a stile, then go along the fenced passage via stiles to a wall-stile into pasture; there is considerable evidence of former quarrying ahead and to the right. Spot the stone marker on the brow of Down Hill and go over the open track rising directly to it, so coming close to the striking section of vallum ditch. The Path drifts leftward via successive stiles onto the verge. Cross the B6318 opposite the entrance to Carr Hill Farm.

10/23

The Portgate ⇄ Heavenfield

*At last the great horizons
of Northumberland and the
North Pennines open to north and south*

Distance: 3.1 miles/5km

◄◄W **WESTBOUND 10** Errington Arms, the pub name, derives from the local land-owning family whose Victorian Gothic home was Beaufront Castle, Hexham. Climb over the ladder-stile into the pasture heading west amid shallow traces of ridge-and-furrow, with the vallum to left. Notice, right, the road-bounding wall with residual Wall-stone. This pasture path runs straight up to a ladder-stile spanning a fence beside the vallum ditch. The top of the stile is a good spot to pause and look back beyond the Errington Arms to Down Hill. A fence excludes the Path from the gorse-filled vallum ditch; note the retaining wall beneath the fence – an unusual feature. At the top of the field cross a stile into a minor road. Turn right in 20 yards to a ladder-stile; after a few yards cross a ladder-stile spanning a light fence, which at this point is parallel with a vernacular stone field barn on Whittington Fell. Several thorn bushes 'hover' close to the vallum. Go through a kissing-gate at the top end of the field into **Stanley Plantation**, a sombre mass of mature conifers. Veer right, then left alongside the roadside wall, several feet below road level.

Pass a redundant Ordnance Survey column, forlorn for want of a lick of white paint. Stand beside it a moment; this the high point of Whittington Fell 879ft/268m. The view north into Northumberland is very extensive. The road stretches away west, as true as an arrow. The Romans were also highly proficient military surveyors – the vallum is parallel within the trees. Maps

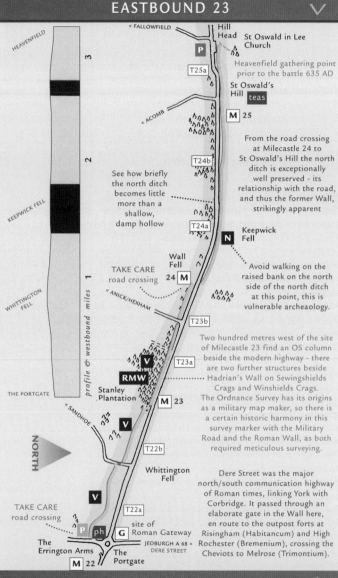

HEAVENFIELD

3

< FALLOWFIELD

Hill Head

St Oswald in Lee Church

Heavenfield gathering point prior to the battle 635 AD

P

T25a

St Oswald's Hill **teas**

M 25

< ACOMB

KEEPWICK FELL

2

T24b

From the road crossing at Milecastle 24 to St Oswald's Hill the north ditch is exceptionally well preserved - its relationship with the road, and thus the former Wall, strikingly apparent

See how briefly the north ditch becomes little more than a shallow, damp hollow

T24a

N Keepwick Fell

Wall Fell

TAKE CARE road crossing

24 **M**

Avoid walking on the raised bank on the north side of the north ditch at this point, this is vulnerable archeaology.

< ANICK/HEXHAM

WHITTINGTON FELL

1

profile & westbound miles

T23b

Two hundred metres west of the site of Milecastle 23 find an OS column beside the modern highway - there are two further structures beside Hadrian's Wall on Sewingshields Crags and Winshields Crags. The Ordnance Survey has its origins as a military map maker, so there is a certain historic harmony in this survey marker with the Military Road and the Roman Wall, as both required meticulous surveying.

V

RMW

T23a

THE PORTGATE

Stanley Plantation

M 23

< SANDHOE

V

NORTH

T22b

Whittington Fell

Dere Street was the major north/south communication highway of Roman times, linking York with Corbridge. It passed through an elaborate gate in the Wall here, en route to the outpost forts at Risingham (Habitancum) and High Rochester (Bremenium), crossing the Cheviots to Melrose (Trimontium).

V

T22a

TAKE CARE road crossing

P ph **G** site of Roman Gateway

The Errington Arms

The Portgate

JEDBURGH A 68 > DERE STREET

M 22

show the Roman Military Way has survived, though brambles discourage investigation.

Exit the plantation via a hand-gate and cross a track to a hand-gate. With a light fence left, and a wall right beside the road, traverse 100 yards of stone flagging at an open section through damp woodland. Leave at a small section of deciduous coppice via a ladder-stile onto the road (signpost Acomb 2; brown signs: hotel 2.25, Camping Site 2.5). From the facing ladder-stile the Path leads through an old quarried patch beside gorse-smothered vallum banks, alive with rabbits – the sandy soils are easily excavated by the rabbits, and the prickles discouraging their arch-enemy, the fox. ▶

Leave the scrub woodland at a stile that leads into open pasture. Advance to a recessed wall step-stile, a refuge for a small party to gather before making a 'well-judged' crossing of the busy race track, the B6318, into the facing farm access to Errington Hill Head. There is a wall-stile, left, before the cattle-grid, guiding walkers down to a fence and on, westward, in pasture beside the north ditch upon **Keepwick Fell**.

After an ash tree, walkers are honour bound to avoid stepping on the pronounced counter-scarp ridge on the north side of the north ditch. This is actually Roman banking from the excavation of the original ditch and is rarely in evidence; it is vulnerable and precious, even though it looks like a simple mounding up of earth! The north ditch gets shallower, becoming a pool as it approaches the open track to Keepwick Farm. Cross over the ladder-stile, continuing beside the north ditch. The road, and thus the base of the Wall, appears higher than the path. The moat of the north ditch is very impressive, one gets an excellent impression of the course of the frontier at this point. A line of beeches on south side of road form their own version of a frontier wall! Look ahead to the scarp and dip hill of Sewingshields Crags, a distant skyline feature due west. Cross a stile tucked under a stately tree. Proceed to a gate in a fence then dip through the north ditch to follow the south side, with gorse smothering the ditch to the right. Notice coir matting giving restorative

Look south-west to get a distant glimpse of Cross Fell, the highest point on the Pennines. The view is, in effect, a grand sweep of the North Pennines Area of Outstanding Natural Beauty.

protection to the eroded scarp bank. The Path leads down to a hand-gate, then a kissing-gate, after the remains of what may have been a pig-sty. Steps lead to the verge in front of terrace at **St Oswald's Hill**, the last house being a tea-room! The farm buildings at the end probably include Wall-stone.

A hand-gate inscribed 'Heavenfield' gives entry into a pasture. Continue beside the road-bounding wall with the church in a walled island over to the right. Reach a gate beside a lay-by. The attendant discursive panel explains the historic significance of this place. The chunky replica wooden cross, erected in 1930 by a group of local people, commemorates the famous Saxon battle that took place here. Going back into prehistory, **Heavenfield** was a meeting of track-ways, on which the Romans superimposed their own military roads and Wall. There is little to suggest to the casual visitor the cultural importance of this ridge-top, other than the enigmatic name.

Heavenfield Cross

ST OSWALD IN LEE

Do visit the little island church of St Oswald in Lee over the molehill-mounded open pasture. The wall and much of the church fabric was constructed from Wall-stone, though the church was completely rebuilt in 1737. Take a moment to look inside and note the large family hatchment on the wall – as it is all black it confirms the husband died after his wife; the Roman altar a little under 5 feet high beside the font – the lettering has gone, but its height suggests that it belonged to an officer of high rank; and within the ante-room, an exhibition prepared by the monks of Lindisfarne. A hand-board shows the content of the wonderfully expansive view obtained from the north side of the churchyard. The church, where once Roman scouts trod, is the spiritual home of the Northumberland Girl Guide Association.

The earliest church lay close to the rallying point of the momentous battle of AD634 between Oswald, the Christian King of Northumbria, and Cadwallon, the heathen leader of British tribes. Prior to this event Northumbria had been divided into two kingdoms, Deira and Bernicia. Deira was ruled by Oswald's uncle, Edwin, converted to Christianity by Paulinus in AD627, whilst Bernicia

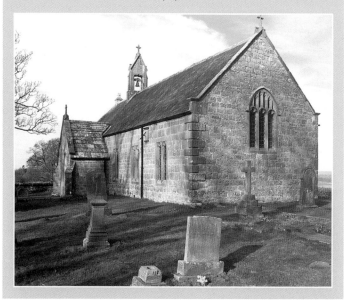

was ruled by Eanfrid, Oswald's brother. Cadwallon made war with Northumbria, confronting and killing Edwin, his son Osric, and Eanfrid, the last two both having renounced Christianity. When Oswald became king he rallied forces and raised a rude wooden cross as a standard, confronting his adversaries south of the Tyne. The Venerable Bede refers to the act of raising the cross as being the first sign of Christianity in Bernicia. Cadwallon was chased and killed on the banks of the Rowley Burn to south of Hexham.

Tradition holds this to have been an important moment for the flowering of Christianity in Britain: the church erected here by the monks of Hexham Abbey became the fountainhead for the proliferation of places of worship throughout the kingdom and beyond. On his death Oswald's head was placed in St Cuthbert's coffin in Durham Cathedral, thus confirming the high esteem in which he was held. A final detail – as you leave the churchyard note the stepped horse-mounting stand, harking back to the days when the preacher and much of the congregation arrived on horse-back.

➡E EASTBOUND 23 From the Heavenfield Cross lay-by, the Path advances inside the field beside the main road to a hand-gate. Pass on in front of the terrace at St Oswald's Hill, via steps to a hand-gate. Now beside the north ditch, slip left through the gorse-choked hollow to a hand-gate. Bear right via a sequence of stiles alongside the north ditch, emerging at the delta exit from Errington Hill Farm. Cross the notoriously fast-track road to the facing recess, continue over a further series of stiles, passing close to the vallum, and emerge at a minor road junction. Continue within a plantation, via a section of stone flags, to a track crossing, then go on within the mature conifer wood of Stanley Plantation. Exit near the vallum and proceed east beside the gorse-covered banking to stiles onto a minor road. Go right some 30 yards then left, over the ladder-stile, continuing beside the vallum fence. After the next ladder-stile, go down open pasture to a ladder-stile into the car park on the south side of the Errington Arms – how convenient!

11/22

Heavenfield ⇄ Chollerford

Down with the Wall, I say;
down to the north Tyne and o'er

Distance: 3.8 miles/6km

◀◀W WESTBOUND 11 Aim part-right, not as currently directed by the wooden sign which was 30 percent out of line (it should now have been correctly aligned). Cross the ladder-stile in the wall corner with the north ditch close right; see the massive burr on the adjacent oak tree. The Path runs gently down through an open wood-cum-pasture to a stile beside a holly bush. Descend the ensuing pasture, and note the north ditch quickly dissolving into the cultivated pasture, its course drifting across the line of the road below **Planetrees** Farm; there is no present evidence of plane trees growing in the vicinity, the trees being distinguished by their height and maple-like leaves. Note the circular 'gin-gang' among the farm buildings: in this device a harnessed horse walked

Broad Wall becomes Narrow Wall at Planetrees

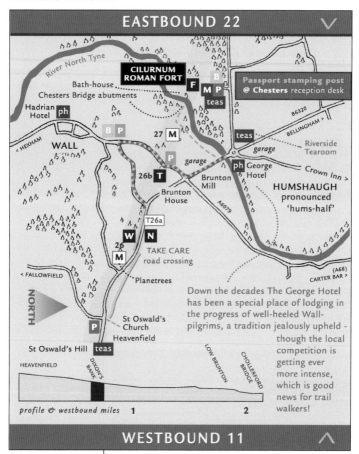

River North Tyne

CILURNUM ROMAN FORT

F

B

M P

Bath-house
Chesters Bridge abutments

teas

Passport stamping post
@ **Chesters** reception desk

Hadrian
Hotel ph

B6320

BELLINGHAM >

B P

WALL

27 M

teas

Riverside
Tearoom

< HEXHAM

P

garage

garage

ph George
Hotel

Crown Inn >

26b T

Brunton
Mill

HUMSHAUGH
pronounced
'hums-half'

Brunton
House

A6079

T26a

W N

< FALLOWFIELD

26
M

TAKE CARE
road crossing

(A68)
CARTER BAR >

Planetrees

NORTH

P

St Oswald's
Church
Heavenfield

St Oswald's Hill teas

HEAVENFIELD

DIXON'S
BANK

LOW BRUNTON

CHOLLERFORD
BRIDGE

Down the decades The George Hotel
has been a special place of lodging in
the progress of well-heeled Wall-
pilgrims, a tradition jealously upheld -
though the local
competition is
getting ever
more intense,
which is good
news for trail
walkers!

profile & westbound miles   1   2

around in a circle, with gearing transferring the power to
a corn mill, which ground oats and barley for stock-feed.
Cross the ladder-stile at the bottom of the next field,
then continue beside the hedge to a stile onto a quarry
access lane.

Go left, crossing the main road to steps down into a
pasture, and angle right to pass the fenced section of

Hadrian's Wall some 40 yards long. In its midst, miraculously surviving, the point where the initial 10-foot Broad Wall changes to the eight-foot-wide Narrow Wall. From this point westward the structure becomes Hadrian's Narrow Wall. Though much of it has the Broad Wall foundations, such evidence clearly shows that these foundations were laid prior to the main building process. This point is significant, as it shows how far the Wall-building process had progressed before this major time- and labour-saving decision was made. ▶

Cross the stile over the wall, below the section with the north ditch becomes a stream hidden behind thicket. Where it re-emerges the path crosses a ladder-stile and enters a woodland strip. In late winter snowdrops predominate; there are also a few floral indicators of ancient woodland such as dog's mercury. The wood opens onto a minor road, where you go left. Note the stone trough in the wall down the lane (difficult to date), which in its time provided refreshment for working horses. See the gazebo in the grounds of **Brunton House**. As you duly meet the main A6097 road, cross carefully into the old road lay-by.

The village of **Wall** lies close left. Follow the footway north, making a diversion at the small lay-by ladder-stile for Brunton Turret; traverse the field below Brunton House to inspect a long stretch of Wall, a further remarkable survival with a deep north ditch. Backtrack, continue upon the footway and notice the staddle stones at Low Brunton Farm, from which the mushroom-shaped capstones are missing. Traditionally set out in grid fashion, planks were laid across the stones, forming a base grid upon which sheaves of corn were placed in layers to be stored as a rick, prior to thrashing; the capstones deterred rodents.

At the **Brunton Watermill** cross-roads go left upon the footway to Chollerford Bridge. (See the old railway station converted to a private home to the right.) The River North Tyne would have been quite shallow in this vicinity – hence the name Chollerford, meaning 'ford in a gorge'. A weir was made here to power a corn mill on the Chesters Estate; the mill building remains.

It was here in 1801 that William Hutton beseeched Henry Tulip, the farmer, not to take any more stones from the Wall for his new farmhouse. The plea went unheeded. A 200 yard section some seven feet high was systematically dismantled, mercifully leaving this precious portion.

Chesters east abutment

River view, North Tyne at Chesters

Chesters west abutment

CHESTERS BRIDGE

Time to consider a detour to inspect Chesters Bridge. Immediately before the road bridge pass through the hand-gate on the left, with an intriguing, surely weighted shutting device. Follow the rather fussily restricted fenced approach path beside the old North Tyne Railway, which ran from Hexham to Bellingham (pronounced bell'in'jum). The Roman bridge abutments and stem Wall lie in a beautifully embowered situation.

There were two bridges, the earlier footbridge superseded by a grander structure sporting a chariot way. There are two interpretative boards offering substantial information. Amongst the features to see are a Roman phallus repelling the evil-eye (a common device on the Wall) and the Roman crane emplacement used to lift the massive limestone blocks with their Lewis-hole slots. Pier masonry dredged from the river lies adjacent.

Through the trees gain a view of the magnificent Chesters bath-house across the river in the parkland of Chesters House. The Roman name for the associated fort was Cilurnum, derived from the Celtic name for the swirling North Tyne river – 'place of the cauldron pool'. One wonders if the river-name Tyne actually meant the forked river, from the meeting of the two main tributaries, North and South Tyne, downstream of this spot near Hexham.

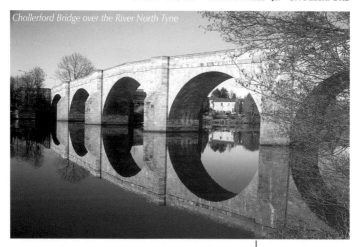
Chollerford Bridge over the River North Tyne

⇥E EASTBOUND 22 An opportunity to visit Chesters Bridge (see opposite). Follow the footway from Chollerford Bridge to the cross-roads at Brunton Watermill; go right, keeping to the footway, taking the opportunity to visit Brunton Turret 26B. Keeping beside the A6097 reach an old road lay-by just short of the village of Wall; carefully cross the road into the by-road. This leads towards the Military Road; only paces short, bear right into the woodland strip (open access point). At the top cross a ladder-stile and continue up the pasture to a stile spanning a field-wall to pass the fine section of Wall with, at its midst, the point of transition from Broad to Narrow Wall. Keep up the pasture to find steps onto the verge of the Military Road; traverse with care, as traffic can come hurtling down at this point! Cross the stile immediately to the right at the quarry access, follow the roadside hedge, via the ladder-stile, and rise up the pasture to the stile beside a holly bush. Continue to a ladder-stile over a wall corner, marching on to the Heavenfield Cross beside the gate access from the lay-by. St Oswald in Lee church, Heavenfield, lies over to the left of an island at the site of the Heavenfield battle of AD635.

12/21

Chollerford ⇄ Tower Tye

*A time of tranquil transition as the route
rises from the amiable environs of Chesters*

Distance: 2.1 miles/3.4km

◄◄W **WESTBOUND 12** Cross Chollerford Bridge. The refuges allow time to pause and gaze upstream at the broad, shallow waters of a stately river lined with trees into the far distance towards Chollerton. However, the flow is periodically bolstered by out-rushes from Kielder Reservoir. Downstream, over the broad, rushing weir, grey heron casually perch and pick choice salmon.

The **George Hotel**, a former coaching inn, stands at an important fork in the way. Northwards the road leads to Bellingham, Kielder and Redesdale; westwards the Military Road forges on to Carlisle. Note the Victorian letter-box set into the facing wall; these are becoming the increasingly rare. The nearby village of Humshaugh is the birth-place of the well-loved contemporary actor Kevin Whateley.

Walkers might make the brief diversion to inspect **Chesters Walled Garden**, with its national collection of marjoram and thyme, but with time at a premium you may wish to forge on up the hill. On the climb from Chesters to Walwick the view south is dominated by Warden Hill, its Iron Age hill-fort one of the largest in northern England and thought to have been something of a fulcrum retreat most actively used prior to the arrival of the Romans. **Walwick**, pronounced 'wolic', means 'the outlying farm on the Roman Wall'. The arch-fronted cottage on the right was formerly a blacksmith's shop – the original forge extant as a striking internal domestic feature. Opposite is the site of **Milecastle 28**. Above Walwick House take the minor road right – a

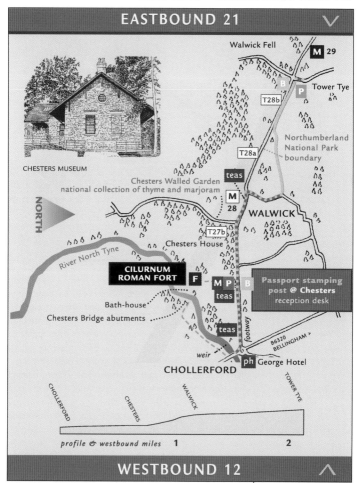

Walwick Fell

M 29

B

P Tower Tye

T28b

Northumberland
National Park
boundary

T28a

teas

Chesters Walled Garden
national collection of thyme and marjoram

M
28

CHESTERS MUSEUM

WALWICK

NORTH

T27b

Chesters House

River North Tyne

**CILURNUM
ROMAN FORT** **F**

M P **B** Passport stamping
post @ **Chesters**
reception desk

teas

Bath-house
Chesters Bridge abutments

teas

footway

B6320
BELLINGHAM >

weir

CHOLLERFORD ph George Hotel

TOWER TYE

CHOLLERFORD

CHESTERS

WALWICK

profile & westbound miles **1** **2**

significant moment, for henceforward the Path never
again has to endure running on, or by, the Military
Road...caveat: the two Brocolitia crossings (see maps
13/20 and 14/19)!

CILURNUM ROMAN FORT AND CHESTERS MUSEM

Chesters Museum

Follow the footway from the roundabout and garage, with its welcome new Riverside Tea-room, and head for the drive entrance to **Chesters Museum**, cared for by English Heritage. This is the most important site actually on the Wall since Segedunum – Corpostopitum at Corbridge is obviously on a par, though not on the Wall itself. It is a famous spot for Wall-pilgrims, with its Clayton connection. The overwhelming majority of exhibits in the outdoor museum of Wall features from along the great Whin Sill ridge to the Cumbrian border have survived only because of John Clayton's enlightened action to preserve the Wall.

From the reception (official National Trail Passport stamping post) make your first port of call the purpose-built fort museum, which is full of stones and artefacts to excite the mind: the inscriptions constitute our formal records from the age of the Roman Wall. Notice the inscribed stone casually lying on the ground at the entrance; sawn from a Roman quarry face on Fallowfield Fell, it refers to Flavius Cauranticus. From the adjacent cafe, Lucullus Larder, advance along the fence passage to make a detailed scrutiny of Cilurnum Roman fort, portions crisply defined by fences within a greater pale. Cattle graze at liberty in the park, ruminating at the paradox of humans thus corralled. The fort rests in an agreeably pastoral setting beside the tree-shaded River North Tyne: clearly in

Stone removed from a quarry on Fallowfield Fell, resting at the door to Chesters Museum – 'to Flavius Curanticus'

view to the south is Warden Hill Iron Age hill-fort, brought under the empire's control.

In its design Cilurnum breaks the mould of Wall forts, which are normally seven miles apart in exposed situations, and is unusual in that the Wall meets the fort plumb in the middle. Its special function was to serve as a cavalry garrison. Hence the appropriateness of the impressive Vanbrugh Baroque courtyard block of Chesters Stud across the road from **Chesters House**.

In 1978 an altar inscribed 'ala aug b virt appel' was discovered, identifying a cavalry called Augusta for Valour, the first regiment to occupy the fort. The Second Cavalry Regiment of Asturians succeeded, and were stationed here for 200 years, during which time they would have lost all trace of their Spanish origins.

Touring the site one quickly recognises that the spacious interior allowed for a generosity in

Cilurnum Bath House

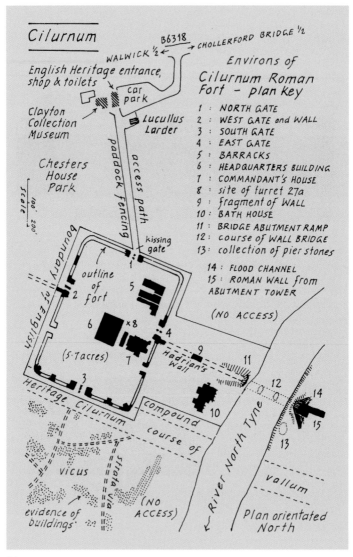

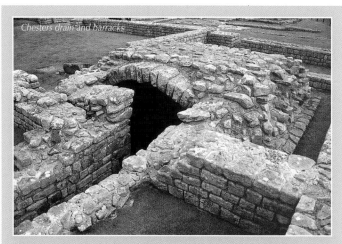
Chesters drain and barracks

the proportions of the buildings. The outline of the fort is poorly represented in the reconstruction. Of the central features, only the north-east barracks, headquarters building with strong-room and the commanding officer's residence remain. John Clayton is known to have found, and promptly back-filled, other elements which appear to have included granaries, workshops and stables. The gates are the exception to the curtain wall deficiency, with both the east and west gates exiting unusually north of the Wall (which is visible). Descending towards the river, pass a fragment of Wall as the ground begins to swell forming the ramp for the great bridge carrying the Military Way high over the river. The second bridge, built *circa* AD208 during the reign of Septimius Severus, was considered to have been the single most impressive component

Cilurnum Commandant's House

bath-house suite backed by the North Tyne

of the entire Wall system. It carried the Military Way, flanked by a parapet decorated with columns and altars. Perhaps the most fascinating component of the site today is the bath-house suite, complete with robe niches (or did the seven alcoves hold deities?), with the evidence of plaster still clinging to the inner walls. You may roam no further; backtrack to the reception and onto the roadside footway.

The country road winds on. Notice the six-foot-tall standing stone in the pasture on the right (no access); as it has no mention on the county 'Sites and Monuments Record' it is not considered old. Find a ladder-stile deporting into a pasture on the left. Advance with a rustic fence, left, in a pasture adored by moles; beyond the tall, remote garden-end wall of Walwick Hall, pass a trough in a broken wall. Continue with a fence left, and when this falters take a shallow left, bearing up to a stile. Follow the headland of arable land to a ladder-stile; to the left is the deep north ditch of the Wall holding a concrete tank. Keep to the right of the old limestone quarry, follow the roadside hedge to a ladder-stile, and continue latterly with a wall, close left, to a ladder-stile precisely on the line of the Wall at the broad road junction at Tower Tye.

↱**E EASTBOUND 21** From the junction verge a ladder-stile on the line of the invisible Wall sets the Path into the pasture. Follow along beside the wall and roadside hedge. Cross a ladder-stile and continue until meeting an old limestone quarry set in the field. Keep to its left-hand side, dipping through the north ditch to reach a ladder-stile. Follow along the headland to a stile, and descend the pasture towards the distant wind turbines on the horizon. At a fence corner continue with the fence right, pass through a broken wall gap by a trough to the ladder-stile onto the minor road, and turn right to enter Walwick. Go left following the footway down the hill; this passes Chesters Stud, the hidden Chesters House and the entrance to Chesters Museum and fort site (English Heritage). Continue to the roundabout and crossing of Chollerford Bridge.

Wall merging into a guardhouse of the west gate

13/20

Tower Tye ⮂ Carrawburgh

Storming along the wall by Limestone Corner to Brocolitia

Distance: 2.1 miles/3.4km

◄◄W WESTBOUND 13 Tower Tye marks the crossing of an old drove route. There are Roman marching camps immediately to the south on Walwick Fell. From here it is only a matter of a further mile to Carr Edge Plantation, with its memorial to Robert Baden Powell's very first Boy Scout holiday camp in 1908. Only eight years previously, during the Boer War, General Baden Powell had distinguished himself at the defence of Mafeking. ◄

From the Tower Tye cross-roads go right, cross to the small lay-by and signed path leading up to a wall backed by young conifers. Follow on right, by a water tank amongst bracken. Curve round the rough bank noting the arrival of the north ditch over the wall. At a stile follow on through the north ditch by the steps and fenced passage. When wet the ground is quite slippery. Emerging from the hand-gate keep up above the square earthworks. This is **Milecastle 29**, palpably vulnerable to damage. Ideally

Tower Tye means 'boundary peel' – the present dwelling, set plumb on the line of Hadrian's Wall, was presumably constituted from a previous rebuild of stout Wallstone. This, in turn, may have replaced an earlier timber dwelling possibly set into the remains of Milecastle 29.

The vulnerable earthen banks of Milecastle 29

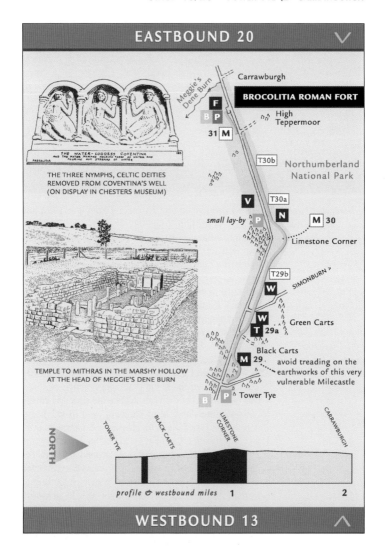

EASTBOUND 20

Carrawburgh

Meggie's Dene Burn

F
B **P**

BROCOLITIA ROMAN FORT

High
Teppermoor

31 **M**

THE THREE NYMPHS, CELTIC DEITIES
REMOVED FROM COVENTINA'S WELL
(ON DISPLAY IN CHESTERS MUSEUM)

T30b

Northumberland
National Park

V **T30a**

P **N**

small lay-by

M 30

Limestone Corner

T29b

W SIMONBURN →

W **T** 29a

Green Carts

Black Carts

M 29

avoid treading on the
earthworks of this very
vulnerable Milecastle

TEMPLE TO MITHRAS IN THE MARSHY HOLLOW
AT THE HEAD OF MEGGIE'S DENE BURN

B **P** Tower Tye

NORTH

TOWER TYE

BLACK CARTS

LIMESTONE CORNER

CARRAWBURGH

profile & westbound miles   1   2

WESTBOUND 13

North ditch engulfed in gorse west of Black Carts

this should fenced off to protect it from farm stock and pedestrian erosion; hopefully, in the future it will be properly excavated and exhibited. The site shows meticulous Roman measuring; but why they did not perch the milecastle on top of the knoll closer to Tower Tye for a better all-round view?

Keep to the roadside wall, and cross the access lane to Black Carts Farm via facing kissing-gates. The term 'carts' comes from 'ceart' meaning 'rocky land'; hence Black Carts meant 'heather fell', while Green Carts meant 'grassy fell'. The path naturally draws up the pasture to inspect a considerable length of consolidated Wall, including **Turret 29a**. This is the longest section thus far. The turret shows the Broad Wall wings, indicating that it was built ahead of the Wall. Notice the slots and curved groove in the slab-footing showing wear from a heavy door hinge. Leave the field, crossing the narrow road by facing wall-stiles. Clamber up the facing bank and after 70 yards rejoin a further stretch of consolidated Wall. The north ditch is a striking feature. Gorse has been trimmed from above the upper section of Wall – watch out for stumps. Just before the remains of an old field-wall crosses the line of the Wall, the north ditch begins to dwindle. It was probably never fully excavated by the Romans, as the bedrock remains undisturbed all the way around what is known as Limestone Corner.

LIMESTONE CORNER

This is Limestone Corner – a real misnomer, as the rock is unforgiving Whinstone. At the centre of the ditch one particularly large rock catches the eye. Spot the six wedge slots in the top, cut by Roman engineers attempting to split the massive block. The vallum had been completed, with the rocks set up on either side of that ditch, but the excavation of the north ditch was halted at this point, in spite of its important defensive role. The problems must have been mounting and discontent rampant – had mutiny been threatened? When the order came forward to cease work there must have been loud cheers and much merriment that night in Brocolitia – perhaps even the officers said their prayers in the *Mithreum* at a calamity avoided. Limestone Corner is the most northerly point on the entire Wall system.

Limestone Corner

The view north reveals a spacious scene down into North Tynedale. Chipchase Castle is prominently in view; this Jacobean mansion was built by Cuthbert Heron in 1621 around a 14th-century peel. The eye is drawn over the spreading hills of Redesdale, beyond Bellingham to the Simonside Hills and the distant Cheviots; this is the upland heartland of Northumberland, beloved of discerning travellers, and much of this area has rightly been designated a national park. This is a land brim-full of ghostly stories, black deeds, pillage and cruel blood feuds from the centuries of unchecked lawlessness. Henry VIII did not ease affairs by his eagerness to keep the 'pot boiling' among these reiver families. He instructed the Duke of Northumberland to slacken his iron hand and 'to let slip them of Tynedale and Redesdale for the annoyance of Scotland'. Not until the Act of Union of 1707 did this sad and over-prolonged embitterment mellow.

THE BORDER REIVERS

While England and Scotland are now at peace, the calm that pervades the Anglo-Scottish Borders was wrought from a cursed age. From the late 13th century until the early 18th century, a fearful cocktail of blood feuding tore the heart out of a huge region from the Tweed and the Tyne to the Nith and the Eden. Spine-chilling tales of reiving raids are a legendary legacy of these violent times, when careless murder, theft and pillage were everyday professions. Retribution and reprisal made no one safe. Lies and deceit were the lethal currency.

Skeletons are to be found in the cupboards of many families whose names persist in the local phone book – Armstrong, Bell, Charlton, Douglas, Elliot, Graham, Irvine, Kerr, Maxwell, Nixon, Robson, Scott, Storey and many more. Reiving lawlessness was eventually stemmed in 1707 by the Act of Union bringing Scotland and England under one crown. However, the term 'reiving' persists in the word 'bereavement'; and from this time too comes the term 'blackmail', an payment extorted for not disclosing a secret. For more information on the reivers, visit the Millennium Gallery at Tullie House, Carlisle, or read *The Steel Bonnets* by George MacDonald Fraser.

Pass a redundant Ordnance Survey pillar amid the untidy evidence of Wall-robbing – though this could equally be the result of lax work from Ministry of Works contractors gathering stone for their consolidated rebuild! The Path crosses a ladder-stile and advances with the shallow ditch until suddenly confronted by huge stones; most lie on the northern lip of the north ditch.

Looking west the north ditch and vallum run in close harmony, sandwiching the 18th-century Military Road, here following the Roman Military Way, though the Wall became subsumed. The Path slips through the north ditch advancing to a stile. Keep along the right-hand side of the north ditch. After two ladder-stiles notice the 'in-filled' north ditch, with the irregular fans of excavated soil from the ditch, settled from Roman times, in the pasture beneath one's feet. A light electric fence keeps farm stock and walkers segregated. Pass Carrawburgh Farm; the name means 'defended place near rocks' – from 'carreg', Celtic for 'rocks'. The rocks referred to can only be those in the Limestone Corner vicinity – there is no other evidence of rock hereabouts.

One more ladder-stile leads on to a light stile onto the lane end to **High Teppermoor** Farm, an enigmatic place-name for which there is no satisfactory explanation – though this in itself suggests it is certainly old. Cross the main road half-left, and a stile steps the walker down into the field on the south side of the road. Go right, keeping out a little way to avoid the old quarried area, advance to a ladder-stile, and maintain a course to meet the path from the car park beside a fence. The car park serves both the site of Brocolitia and the *Mithreum*, but there are no other facilities.

↦E EASTBOUND 20 The Path breaks from the fort-side fence to a ladder-stile over a fence then skirts a shallow former quarry to reach a step-stile onto the main road. Go half-left into the entrance to High Teppermoor Farm. Go immediately right, over the stile and follow the north ditch by a sequence of three ladder-stiles. After a further stile the Path slips through the north ditch passing the rocky section at Limestone Corner. The rocks quickly abate. The Path keeps by the shallow north ditch and, crossing a ladder-stile, passes an old Ordnance Survey column. Descend beside a rubble rigg, showing signs of crude robbing, to two neat sections of consolidated wall. Cross the minor road by facing wall-stiles, and continue down by the fine stretch of Wall which includes Turret 29a. Drift to the right-hand corner and cross the lane to Black Carts Farm by facing kissing-gates. Keep beside the roadside wall, passing above the earthen remains of Milecastle 29. A hand-gate gives entry into a fenced passage and steps through the north ditch, then over the stile. Keep the wall close right, and curve round beside the conifer copse to meet the road.

14/19

Carrawburgh ⇄ Sewingshields Farm

*Beside the north ditch heading
assuredly towards the Whin Sill scarp*

Distance: 2.1 miles/3.4km

◄◄W WESTBOUND 14 The high earthen banks of **Brocolitia Roman fort** are clearly in view over the fence, to casual eyes looking like an Iron Age encampment. The fort-name means 'hill above the badger's sett', another example of the Romans adopting an element from local language. Follow the pathway, rounding the fence corner, and bear right down the bank towards the ***Mithreum*** enclosure. The *Mithreum* has many visitors – some come to investigate its purpose, while others come to worship in their own way; hence the occasional offerings of coins and other artefacts that appear on the trio of replica altars. Located in

Mithreum at Brocolitia

Sewingshields Farm

track to Stell Green

Sewingshields Castle (motte)

T 34a
Sewingshields

school-house

RMW

old telephone exchange
converted into a walkers'
bunkhouse lodgings.

M 34 Grindon - in a walled plantation

Hadrian Lodge Hotel <
2 miles

T 33b Coe Sike

N

Fozy Moss - *mire*

T33a

V

M 33 vulnerable wall, with
platform protecting west
side of exposed monument.

NORTH ▶

Shield on
the Wall Dam

T32b

N

area of Roman quarries

T32a

Northumberland
National Park

The section from Carraw
to Sewingshields accompanies the
north ditch, frequently as a strikingly
deep feature. This needs to be
respected every bit as much as
any stretch of stone Wall.

V

M 32

P

Carraw is a Celtic word meaning 'at the
rocks', though there are precious few to see!
Formerly there was a peel tower here and it
too has gone without trace.

Carraw Farm

T31b

T31a

Coventina's Well

**BROCOLITIA
ROMAN FORT**

Mithreum

t

F **P**
B

Carrawburgh

CARRAWBURGH

CARRAW

SHIELD IN
THE WALL

SHIELD IN
THE WALL

profile & westbound miles   1   2

a marshy hollow it was only discovered in 1949. Above it lay the civilian settlement (*vicus*). A flagged path leads on to a ladder-stile, with more flagging crossing the wet marsh area of Meggie's Dene Burn.

Go right from the ensuing stile, and pass the rush-filled springs where the Celtic deity Coventina was worshipped by the Romans. When excavated **Coventina's Well** was found to hold the most enormous hoard of offerings, including 22 altars and in excess of 16,000 coins covering the full period of Roman occupation. (There were so many coins, in fact, that one local lad, now in his 90s, remembers being given handfuls of them, which he and chums used as skimming stones on Park Dam on their way home.) Coventina's original shrine stone can be seen in Chesters Museum. The well was discovered accidentally by lead miners during prospecting work in 1876. Note the officers had a masculine temple, *Mithric,* while the soldier of lower rank held a feminine

Looking east from the walled plantation at Milecastle 34

temple, *Coventina*. If nothing else, it does show the pre-disposition of humanity to spiritual observance.

The path crosses a double flagged causeway and the shallow line of the vallum, which curiously ran under the site of Brocolitia, proving that the fort was an after-thought to fill in a long gap between Cilurnum and Vercovicium. Cross the ladder-stile and the main road into the lane entrance, taking the first ladder-stile on the left; keep up by the shallow north ditch. Advance to a stone trail-marker, directing right, to round the corner of the plantation. Stone flags run alongside this sycamore shelter belt behind Carraw Farm, the air rent with the noisy calls from a rookery. **Carraw Farm** was once cen-tred upon a peel tower.

From the next ladder-stile veer left back to resume the walk westward alongside the north ditch, with the wood and scarp of Sewingshields directly ahead. After another ladder-stile the pasture deteriorates to rough grazing. The north ditch attracts attention; notice how the vallum banking over the road appears as though it may have been even higher than the Wall. There is more bulky soil banking on the north side of the north ditch – here not dispersed. Stone flags draw the Path through the north ditch; ignore the inviting ladder-stile, this only connects to a path on the vallum. Keep beside the wall as it begins to create an enclosure alongside the Military Road.

What you are witnessing is the point where the 18th-century road builders veered from the line of the Wall. They never again sacrificed the Wall, or its course, en route to Carlisle. Hence beneath our feet the remains of the Wall continue as a low rubble bank beside the field-wall. A moment of excitement is the site of Milecastle 33, with a small portion of Wall and the north gate; a plat-form protects the west side from foot wear. Bracken defines the remainder of the milecastle over the fence. ▶ Soon after the next ladder-stile the field-wall ends, the Path advances across a dip, where the Military Road cuts through the vallum over to the left.

Advance to **Coe Sike**, Turret 33b, with Broad Wall wings, an internal platform base but no evidence of the

Notice the Shield-on-the-Wall Dam, a stocked private fly-fishery. On my visit two anglers were casting from its midst.

*Sewingshields
Turret 34a*

door; this was blocked in the latter half of the second century. Though originally recessed into the Wall, this too was modified to strengthen the Wall: this in-fill has slumped. The Path marches on to flags passing a walled enclosure filled with sycamore, this is **Milecastle 34**. A sheep creep (low hole in the wall) gave lambs entry for sheltered grazing, and wing walls give stock wind breaks. It is unfortunate that the milecastle was ruined by such a thoughtless planting. Notice in Fozy Moss, just to the north, a medieval ring-and-bailey feature resting upon a slight knoll amongst the rough moor grass and marsh: a summer 'holm' for a wary shepherd conscious of thieves. Shortly after crossing a wall-stile is **Turret 34a**; here there is evidence of the doorway and some internal floor surface as well as what appears to be a thickening of the Wall from when the turret was taken down.

The view from here shows Wark Forest and the distant farmstead of Stell Green. Crossbills frequent the sheltering trees, while in the foreground below are the bare motte earthworks of **Sewingshields Castle**.

As the Path passes a single-storey dwelling it crosses the rough track which is Stell Green's umbilical cord to the outside world.

SEWINGSHIELDS CASTLE

Romantic writers have embroidered Arthurian legend around this 'moss' castle, suggesting that King Arthur hid with Queen Guinevere and their entourage in a cave on Sewingshields Crags waiting for ritual release from their entranced state (hence King's Wicket above Busy Gap, see section 15 (westward)). The site of this steading, complete with fish ponds and moat, was relinquished around the middle of the 16th century. Blooms of cotton grass characterise the quality of the fragile and nationally important habitat of the surrounding raised mires with their associated flora and fauna.

↦E EASTBOUND 19 Cross the open track, glancing by the bungalow to the low ridge, location of Turret 34a, and cross the adjacent wall-stile. The Path follows the north ditch passing the wooded Milecastle 34, on stone flags, then Turret 33b before slipping over the Coe Sike dip to accompany the field-wall, upon the line of the Wall, to a platform crossing the western wall of Milecastle 33.

Keep beside the field-wall until, coming close to the Military Road, the path is ushered left through the north ditch via flags and along the north side of the north ditch, crossing one ladder-stile *en route* to Carraw. A stone marker guides left of the sycamore plantation to a ladder-stile and along the flagged path close to the fence. At the end veer half-right to resume beside the north ditch. Descend to a ladder-stile into a broad lane. Go right, carefully crossing the Military Road to a ladder-stile, then advance via a flagged path into the rush-filled hollow of Meggie's Dene Burn, site of Coventina's Well. The marsh is crossed via stiles and flagging glancing by the *Mithreum* enclosure rising by the fenced Brocolitia Roman fort; a grass-covered earthwork is all that can be seen. Go round the fence corner with the path that leads towards the car park. Watch for the acorn on the fence pin-pointing where the Path breaks east towards a ladder-stile in a fence.

15/18

Sewingshields Farm ⇄ Housesteads

*The dramatic view of the Wall
riding high on the crest of the Whin
Sill wave becomes a breathtaking reality*

Distance: 2 miles/3.2km

◄W **WESTBOUND 15** The path enters Sewingshields Wood via a hand-gate; here you walk upon a bed of bark. The path has a new gravel bed and retaining edge where it glances by Sewingshields Farm; the last little shed, known locally as a 'netty', is a privy with seat *in situ*.

The Path leaves the woodland by a hand-gate to unite with a fine, if intermittent, length of consolidated Wall. A medieval stone grave survives next to the Wall-footing some 50 yards short of **Milecastle 35**. This milecastle did not serve the usual function: a north gate was not created as the escarpment rendered progress to the north impossible; it can have been no more than a glorified watch-tower with auxiliaries lodgings. Within the walls was evidence of timber 'shielings', the medieval summer lodgings of a shepherding family; perhaps they were connected with 'Sigewine', identified in the name Sewingshields.

The walk is well and truly elevated onto the Whin Sill scarp. This is formed from a dense magma known as dolerite intruded as a sheet between layers of carboniferous limestone, shale and sandstone –

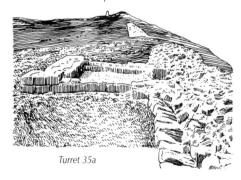

Turret 35a

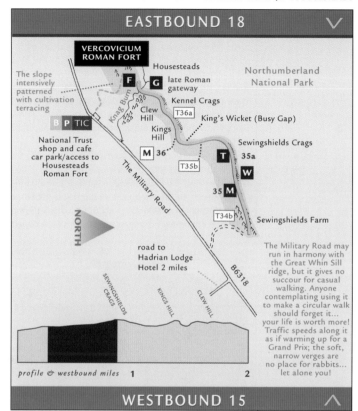

VERCOVICIUM ROMAN FORT

Housesteads

Northumberland National Park

The slope intensively patterned with cultivation terracing

F **G** late Roman gateway

Kennel Crags

Clew Hill

T36a King's Wicket (Busy Gap)

Kings Hill

Sewingshields Crags

B **P** TIC

National Trust shop and cafe car park/access to Housesteads Roman Fort

M 36

T 35a

T35b

W

M 35

The Military Road

NORTH

T34b Sewingshields Farm

road to Hadrian Lodge Hotel 2 miles

B6318

The Military Road may run in harmony with the Great Whin Sill ridge, but it gives no succour for casual walking. Anyone contemplating using it to make a circular walk should forget it... your life is worth more! Traffic speeds along it as if warming up for a Grand Prix; the soft, narrow verges are no place for rabbits... let alone you!

SEWINGSHIELDS CRAGS KINGS HILL CLEW HILL

profile & westbound miles 1 2

hence the name Sill. The landmass has been subsequently tilted, creating the characteristic scarp/dip slope rolling scenery. The dolerite came from a volcano that was active some 295 million years ago located somewhere near the present Cheviot hills. The rock is patterned with joints that have given rise to columns.

Nearing the high point pass **Turret 35a**, showing the door-curved hinge slot and an odd gap through the Wall. The craggy scarp arrives at a brilliant white Ordnance Survey pillar. Though the column's original purpose, map triangulation, has gone, it shows the startling effect of lime-wash. For centuries used on farm dwellings in this area, lime-wash was probably first introduced by the Romans, perhaps as an impressive facing to the Wall itself. The high point provides a superb viewpoint overlooking Broomlee Lough (lake) backed by wave upon wave of scarp hills. In Roman times the poor grassland leading towards the dark horizon of Wark Forest would have been covered with scrub oak, alder, birch and willow. ◄

Note: the wind can be strong at this point.

A final portion of Wall foundation draws into the field-wall which leads on down the scarp edge in a southerly direction. Pass through a hand-gate in the Busy Gap depression; the hand-gate on the rise is known as **King's Wicket** – a reference to King Arthur. The causeway leading north through the moss was an ancient thorough-

Kings Hill

fare. In medieval times people of a thieving disposition entered Tynedale via this route. These 'moss troopers' were known as Busy Gap Rogues, a moss trooper being an inhabitant of this wild mire country. The path slips over **King's Hill** beside the trimly crafted field-wall, into the next dip and up over Clew Hill, with a more serious descent. The last hill is Kennel Crags, which means 'the slope clear of scrub', an accurate description to this day. A ladder-stile puts the Path into a mixed coppice tapering to the pointed wall corner. Clamber over the step-stile beside a majestic Clayton dry-stone reconstruction of the Roman Wall.

Descend into the Knag Burn valley, arriving at the late Roman gateway flanked by guard-rooms. This appears to have be inserted after the fort's north gate was closed and may have mixed military purpose with civilian. Downstream, note a small fenced area; this was a Roman well. Further on, set into the slope is the only Roman lime-kiln to have been discovered. It is interesting to realise that this technique and structural detail was replicated in 19th-century lime-kilns; one may wonder why it took so long to re-invent for 'soil sweetening' purposes. Bearing in mind the sheer quantity of mortar needed to create the Wall there must have been many more lime-kilns dotted around the area, with its copious supplies of timber and coal for fuel.

↞**E EASTBOUND 18** From the Knag Burn gateway turn up left beside the Wall to a wall-stile leading into the tapered end of a mixed plantation. The path weaves through to a ladder-stile and accompanies the neatly coursed field-wall upon the ridge-line of the Roman Wall. Climbing the steep bank onto Clew Hill, through the next gap up onto King's Hill, the ridge turns north, dipping via Busy Gap to a hand-gate then on up the snaking ridge to the crest of Sewingshields Crags. Pass the OS pillar, follow the consolidated Wall by Turret 35a and Milecastle 35, and enter Sewingshields Wood at a hand-gate. Pass through, along the declining ridge by the farm – first upon a gravel, then a bark surface – and exit via a hand-gate.

16/17

Housesteads ⮀ Steel Rigg

*An open-air museum come to life;
all huff and puff along the ridge*

Distance: 3.1 miles/5 km

◀W WESTBOUND 16 While the Path goes on through the hand-gate in the Roman gate to mount the bank beside the Wall, and runs along the northern face of the fort by its monumentally stepped north gate, walkers are encouraged to make a proper inspection of Housesteads, the Vercovicium Roman fort. This is the most inspirational and impressive Wall fort on open exhibition. It was garrisoned by 1000 Tungarian infantry from the modern Belgium, so they were well attuned to walking in this climate.

Bastle in the south gate

Veer half-left, noticing the metal fence some 100 yards down the Knag Burn, this is the site of a Roman

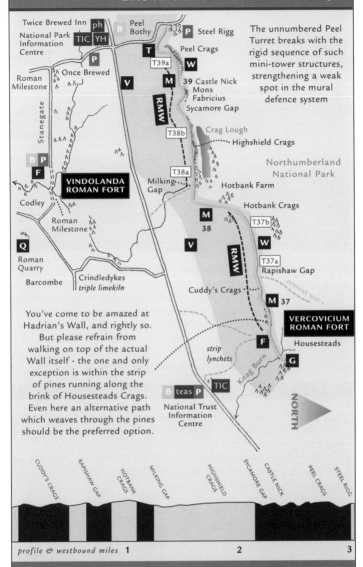

Twice Brewed Inn ph Peel Bothy
National Park TIC YH B P Steel Rigg
Information Centre
P Once Brewed T Peel Crags
Roman Milestone T39a W
V M 39 Castle Nick
Stanegate RMW Mons
Fabricius
Sycamore Gap
B P T38b Crag Lough
F Highshield Crags
VINDOLANDA Northumberland
ROMAN FORT T38a National Park
Codley Milking Hotbank Farm
Gap
Roman Hotbank Crags
Milestone M T37b
Q 38
Roman V RMW W
Quarry T37a
Barcombe Crindledykes Rapishaw Gap
triple limekiln
Cuddy's Crags PENNINE WAY
M 37
You've come to be amazed at VERCOVICIUM
Hadrian's Wall, and rightly so. F ROMAN FORT
But please refrain from Housesteads
walking on top of the actual G
Wall itself - the one and only
exception is within the strip strip
of pines running along the lynchets
brink of Housesteads Crags. Knag Burn
Even here an alternative path B teas P TIC NORTH
which weaves through the pines
should be the preferred option. National Trust
Information
Centre

The unnumbered Peel
Turret breaks with the
rigid sequence of such
mini-tower structures,
strengthening a weak
spot in the mural
defence system

profile & westbound miles   1   2   3

CUDDY'S CRAGS RAPISHAW GAP HOTBANK CRAGS MILKING GAP HIGHSHIELD CRAGS SYCAMORE GAP CASTLE NICK PEEL CRAGS STEEL RIGG

Wall traversing the Knag Burn valley

well. The green path leads up to round the east and southern sides of the fort where it crosses the area of the *vicus* (civilian settlement), to reach the English Heritage reception and museum – an entry fee, essential to visit the real meat and matter of the monument- the internal features of the fort. All down the bank from the fort lies the most amazing collection of cultivation terracing: intensive corn production to fill the fort's *horreum*.

VERCOVICIUM ROMAN FORT

A confusing mix of Romano-British, Saxon and medieval cultivation continuity is present here on one south-facing slope. Cultivation was probably established in the late third century to supplement the fort's store of wheat. This five-star, five-acre sloping site contains a central headquarters building (*principia*), commanding officer's house (*praetorium*), twin barrack blocks, a hospital, latrines, granaries, stout gates and watchtower features.

The south gate includes a medieval bastle (pronounced 'bassul'). Fortunately, the Roman focus of the excavators did not prevent them from keeping this adaptation, made some 1000 years later, though other elements of the medieval farm within the fort were swept away to reveal the Roman

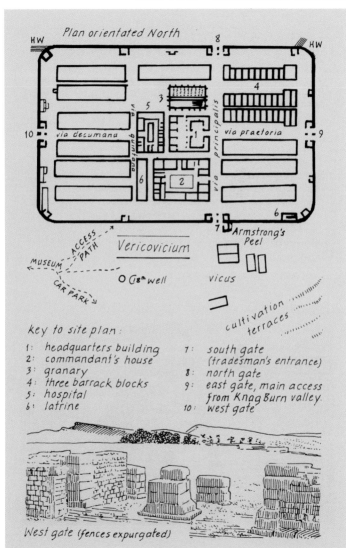

Plan orientated North

HW

8

HW

via decumana

via quintana

3

5

1

4

via principalis

via praetoria

10

9

6

2

6

7

Armstrong's Peel

ACCESS PATH

Vericovicium

MUSEUM

O C18th well

vicus

CAR PARK

cultivation terraces

key to site plan:

1: headquarters building
2: commandant's house
3: granary
4: three barrack blocks
5: hospital
6: latrine

7: south gate
   (tradesman's entrance)
8: north gate
9: east gate, main access
   from Knag Burn valley.
10: west gate

West gate (fences expurgated)

components. William Camden, visiting the area in the 1580s, was warned to keep well clear of the Armstrongs, fierce moss troopers who lived in the bastle. The tiered central accommodation of the fort is impressive, with hypocaust confirming the commanding officer's slightly more luxurious residence. The upper building, comprising the granaries (*horreum*), reveals stone plinths; these held a flagged floor which encouraged ventilation in order to prevent the grain from heating up and spoiling with fungus, a practice still necessary in modern agriculture. A Roman army marched on its stomach, and bread was the basis of its diet.

The communal conclusion of all this eating, the latrines, down in the south-east corner of the fort, are remarkably complete, and quite the best example of such a functional building in Britain. 'Now I don't want you to get the wrong end of the stick' – this phrase comes down to us from the Roman use of personal toiletry sticks with a sponge tied to one end for the purpose of…well, I won't say quite what! The sponge was imported from the Mediterranean, while the lower orders used moss! Roman latrines did not have the benefits of a 'u' trap, so many valuables ended up in the spoils, which is good news for field archaeology!

Super duper latrines at the south-east corner of Vercovicium

One can rejoin the Path from the vicinity of the museum by wandering up by the west side of the fort to a hand-gate. This is a good place to note the fort's rounded corners – apparently the Wall had to be demolished and the fort inserted, hence the slight forward position of the north wall.

When first constructed, it was thought that the Stanegate fort at Vindolanda would serve well enough. But it was soon apparent that the garrison needed to be quick off the mark – a fast-response force to react to spontaneous rebel gatherings was needed. The time and effort lost in getting up the mile of fell-side was considerable and costly in terms of effectiveness. The implanting of forts bang on the Wall made the frontier a working success; Brocolitia actually rests upon the vallum, which had to be filled in to construct the fort.

Aesica, the next fort westward, had a major water sourcing problem. The solution was a six-mile-long aqueduct snaking across the shallow slopes in what were termed 'the barbarian' lands to the north of the Wall. Clearly, preventing sabotage to this head of water was a significant task at Great Chesters.

However, let's be gone. Immediately there is a choice. A nice bark-bedded path weaves through the pine grove of Housesteads Wood or, on this one occasion, a Wall-walk is officially condoned. The Clayton Wall has been specially reinforced to allow visitors to stride upon a gravelled surface and sense the Wall patrol. However, archaeological thinking moves on, and it is now considered a misconception that a patrol walkway ran along the top of the Wall behind crenellations. On purely aesthetic grounds this is a lovely moment, satisfying an urge many people have to walk upon the Wall. At one brief moment walkers with a head for heights, step aside onto the top of a basalt pinnacle to feel the exposure of the cliff-top setting into a biting northerly breeze. The two paths meet to exit at a hand-gate.

Milecastle 37 is rather special; the arched span of the north gate has partially survived, showing the character of these controls limiting the height of traffic.

JOHN CLAYTON

For the first time we encounter Clayton Wall in its basic form. John Clayton of Chesters House devoted every Monday of his professional working life as a lawyer and Town Clerk in Newcastle to the Wall. He employed William Tailford as his foreman for purely Wall excavation and reconstruction tasks. That we have Roman stone walling here at all is due to this one man's classical education and passion alone. Notice how the Wall occasionally steps in and out, a curious detail possibly done just to affirm the work of Tailford's team.

The Military Way, which began from the west gate of the Vercovicium, is seen to contour – and is popularly used by visitors as an alternative green trod to effect a circular walk west of the fort. The trail here traverses a depression by the use of neatly pitched boulder steps.

The Path slips through the 'nick without a name' and climbs onto **Cuddy's Crag**. Was the medieval shepherd here called Cuthbert, as this is the pet-form of the name? The next notch in the ridge is defended by a ragged Whin Sill crag, the path veering left to enter **Rapishaw Gap**. Wild chives is one plant the Romans brought; it still

Milecastle 37 with partial archway in north gate

Housesteads Crag from Cuddy's Crags

tenuously flourishes upon such outcrops, the soil suiting it well, its medicinal value being to inhibit the passing of urine – perhaps useful to keep a sentry 'on watch' alert. This is where the Pennine Way departs from the Wall heading for Wark Forest and the distant Cheviots.

Cross the ladder-stile, and walk alongside a fine stretch of gently undulating Clayton Walling passing the sites of two lost turrets. As Winshields Crags comes into view ahead, a branch path bears half-left above a walled plantation on **Hotbank Crags**. 'Hot' meant 'a ring of trees' – might this imply a religious site or the surrounds to a (now lost) Roman lime-kiln? As the Wall shapes to descend there is the most superb view west to Crag Lough overlooked by Highshield Crags, then to Peel and Winshields Crags. Remember to help conserve the Wall by resisting the temptation of clambering onto the wall to get a better photo. The dry-stone Wall is vulnerable. Looking northwards one can see Greenlee Lough beyond West Hotbanks Farm; this is the largest body of freshwater in Northumberland and is a National Nature Reserve owned by the Northumberland National Park. The Path sweeps down to a ladder-stile and over the sensitive earthen banks of **Milecastle 38**, parallel with **Hotbank Farm**. Again the view to Crag Lough will cause many a

Clayton Wall en route to Rapishaw Gap

camera to emerge from the pack. Continue beside what is now a field-wall bending right to a ladder-stile into **Milking Gap**; the farm-access track slices through a natural nick in the scarp. The gap-name alludes to the historic use of this one weakness in the Sill by cattle drovers. The Military Way is seen a little to the left, while in the rough pasture towards the Military Road large boulders may be detected – survivors from a homestead, probably from the period immediately after the withdrawal of Roman jurisdiction.

Top of Highshield Crags

Cross the facing ladder-stile and follow the field-wall; beyond the north ditch alder carr leads to the shores of **Crag Lough**. A ladder-stile puts the Path into the pine wood, and the Path rises to emerge on the top of **Highshield Crags**. This is a marvellously airy belvedere, with Once Brewed coming into view down to the left. Walkers lacking a head for heights will find the sneaky gully views beneath their feet a bit daunting; others will be ecstatic. Hotbank Crags are now seen to perfection above the choppy waters of Crag Lough, where a pair of swans can be seen elegantly gliding, and fly fishermen in boats try to hook brown trout. The surrounding marshes are ecologically important for pond-weed and fresh water invertebrates. The backing moors are a haven for Curlew, a bird that features as the Northumberland National Park emblem, though here it is sometimes rivalled in early May by the look-alike Whimbrel. The calls are quite different – in fact the latter means 'whimper'; the Curlew's evocative cries are quite the reverse.

On passing a tall section of consolidated Wall, glance right to view a notable pinnacle arete – impressive stuff. Crossing a ladder-stile the Path winds down a newly paved way. The reconstructed Wall is quite massive, and on the south side Broad Wall foundations are visible. The

Wall rising onto Mons Fabricius from Sycamore Gap

mature sycamore gives this next nick its familiar name, **Sycamore Gap**. However, ever since Kevin Cosner in the film 'Robin Hood, Prince of Thieves' rode here to rescue a boy up a tree, it has gained the nickname Robin Hood's Gap. A small walled enclosure attempts to protect a replacement tree; this suffers from frequent wall collapses and will do little better than come up as a small shrub.

The real interest in the gap is what lies under the mature tree. When this eventually dies archaeologists will have access to the mass of rubble beneath it; as excavation techniques are always improving there should be no rush. What is revealed on the north face gives a clue to the merit of careful digging. The Wall here is original, seven courses high – a rare instance of a decent height of undisturbed authentic Roman building, with several black Whinstones incorporated. Whin Sill rock was used only in the lower courses because it was too hard to quarry; hence only easily obtained surface rock found a place in the Wall. The overwhelming majority of the stone was quarried, cut and drawn to the site by horses with waggons or sledges.

It is worth mentioning that, for all the brilliance of the Whin Sill as a natural line for the frontier, the Romans would not have built here but for the presence of limestone. The local carboniferous geological succession also gave them coal to burn the limestone to create the most fundamental ingredient for the entire Wall-building process, mortar. Stone blocks have been laid to effect steps up the steep bank onto the next top, **Mons Fabricius**. Notice the off-set Broad Wall foundation edging stones and a little way along the base of two double-roomed shielings. The medieval shepherds needed the hilltop site and the then substantial Roman Wall as double indemnity from sheep thieves; these moss troopers were as just as likely to kill as to rob.

The Path sweeps down into **Castle Nick**; the milecastle is a square peg in a square hole. Being so close to Steel Rigg many walkers come this way, putting pressure on the surrounding sward; so minimise wear by taking a wide berth and skirt around. Grazing livestock are excluded by means of a stile; the interior of **Milecastle 39** does not give cause to enter.

The Path climbs again, soon accompanying just a rubble bank to a ladder-stile in a dip. The Clayton Wall resumes; it is adorned with a swastika stone, an ancient symbol of good fortune, now matched by the luck in finding it! The dry-stone walling falters approaching the ladder-stile and steep descent into Peel Gap. The way down includes two narrow squeezes, one through the Sill and the second through a low wall-stile. Flagging spans the gap beside the foundations of an out-of-sequence turret. A constant flow of water drains through the wall from the rush-filled marshes in front of **Peel Crags**. These crags are popular with rock-climbers, and one pinnacle catches the eye, having the appearance of an American Indian totem, capped with a brave's head! ◀

An inviting ladder-stile gives access to the road beside Peel Bothy, a Landmark Trust holiday-letting opened by Her Majesty the Queen Mother in 1989.

The road offers a quick way down to Once Brewed National Park Centre, the youth hostel and to the Twice Brewed Inn. These curious names intrigue visitors. Twice Brewed derives from the construction of the Military Road, when a farmer spotted an entrepreneurial opportunity and established a small brewery to slake the thirst of the road navvies and new passing traffic. The custom proved greater than expected, demand outstripping supply, so he watered down the beer. His customers, with due indignation, demanded it was brewed again – hence Twice Brewed! With the establishment of the neighbouring youth hostel, Lady Trevelyan of Wallington Hall (a National Trust property) was invited to formally open the building. Being staunchly temperance she accepted with the proviso that only tea and non-alcoholic beverages would ever be served – so 'once brewed' will always be the order of the day.

From the National Park Centre at Once Brewed walkers can join the Hadrian's Wall Bus to visit Vindolanda. Vindolanda pre-dates the Wall so is not on the actual line of the Path. However, it is a 'must', as it is the very best contemporary exhibition of Roman Wall life and times.

The Path continues up beside the Clayton Walling to a hand-gate and beyond to a wall-stile onto the road close to the **Steel Rigg car park** – the name means 'pointed ridge', descriptive of the short spur just ascended.

↠E EASTBOUND 17 Cross the road by facing wall-stiles and follow the Clayton Wall via a hand-gate down into Peel Gap; here flags lead across a stream. Climb the steep edge of Peel Crags via stiles and keep alongside the ridge-top Wall, dipping by a ladder-stile and continuing initially by a Wall rubble bank. The path sweeps around Milecastle 39 and up onto Mons Fabricius then steeply down into Sycamore Gap. Cross over the Wall in the gap and follow the winding flag-path up onto the crest of Highshield Crags via a ladder-stile. Enter a pine wood, declining to a ladder-stile then alongside a field-wall with the alder carr of Crag Lough close left. Cross the access track to Hotbanks Farm via facing ladder-stiles and follow the field-wall as it bends north, confined by a fence on the right. Slip through the earthworks of unexcavated Milecastle 38 beside Hotbank Farm. Cross a ladder-stile, ascend the bank and resume company with a tangible Clayton Wall over Hotbanks Crags.

Wander along the ridge to dip into Rapishaw Gap via a ladder-stile. The path veers right to avoid shattered outcropping of Whin Sill on the east side of the gap; the original Wall must have been impressive to cope with this sharp dip. Traverse Cuddy's Crags (ahead is the famous view of Housesteads Crag), angling through a depression onto the ridge leading by Milecastle 37. Enter the pine wood along the top of Housesteads Crags; either step onto the Wall-walk or thread through the trees from the hand-gate. Upon exiting the wood either go right, via the hand-gate, to Housesteads Museum or keep to the trail. The Trail steps down left following the narrow grassy ledge along the northern front of the fort. Bear down beside the Wall as it springs from the rounded north-eastern corner of the fort to pass through the Knag Burn Roman gateway.

17/16

Steel Rigg ⇄ Cawfields Quarry

The highest station and the greatest views –
does it get any better? We'll see…

Distance: 3 miles/5km

◄◄W WESTBOUND 17 Crossing the minor road via the facing wall-stiles. The Path begins the steady ascent to **Winshields Crags**, the highest point on the Whin Sill and, therefore, on the entire National Trail. Through a gateway, with a field-wall to the right and the north ditch beyond, rise to a hand-gate: keen eyes might notice not only the Military Way emerging from the left but a small grassy rectangle adjacent to the field-wall, another unexcavated medieval shieling. Directly above the hand-gate a platform gives a clue to the site of **Milecastle 40**, the fenced gap further emphasising its position; some loose stones lie on the east side. ◄

The Wall as it continues is quite uncharacteristic of any other Wall rebuild – more akin to vertical crazy paving. The Wall foundations make an early presage for a short resumption of consolidated Wall; only on the last step to the summit does field-wall begin, and then fencing, at the broad space alongside the old Ordnance Survey column.

In the immediate country to the north below this great scarp lie a dozen farmsteads, which originally would have been summer shielings, spread out, in typical Scandinavian fashion, equidistant across a broad, low moorland vale. From this spot the sense of being above, and yet within, a breathing landscape is profound. During the ascent from the Military Road the gusting winds appear to have blow the 'd' out of the hill-name – hence we have Winshields Crag and Windshields Farm.

In the very next dip a wooden sign directs a footpath down the dry valley to Windshields Farm, a useful

Some 20 years ago a telescope stood here giving the energetic visitor the opportunity to gaze at a marvellous panorama. The view stretches from Cross Fell, the highest summit in the Pennine chain within the North Pennines Area of Outstanding Natural Beauty, down to the south; and extends to the northern horizon, limited by the Border Forests of Wark, →

profile ↔ westbound miles

1

2

3

< GREENHEAD

Haltwhistle Burn

Burnhead

Northumberland National Park

P

Cawfields Quarry Picnic Site

Milecastle Inn

B ph

C

C

marching camps

Stanegate

WINSHIELDS CRAGS

BOGLE HOLE

CAW GAP

THORNY DOORS

CAWFIELDS QUARRY

B6318

M 42

Cawfields Farm

Cawfields Crags

V

RMW

T41b

Thorny Doors

T 41a

tiny section of north ditch at this point

Shield on the Wall Farm

M 41

Caw Gap

Bogle Hole

RMW

Sook Hill

V

Melkridge Common

T40b

NORTH ▶

Lodhams Slack

Winshields Crags

1132ft/345m

V

Green Slack

T40a

Vindolanda Stanegate Fort thoroughly merits a visit. Walk, Bus or Drive it is only 1.4 miles from Once Brewed, accessed via a classic stretch of Stanegate.

Windshields Farm

camping site

M 40

shieling

RMW

N

Twice Brewed Inn ph

Vallum Lodge

Steel Rigg

Once Brewed National Park Information Centre

P YH

Springwell Cottage

P

B

< VINDOLANDA

Peel Bothy

← Spadeadam and Kielder. Westward gaze into Scotland to Criffel, across the Solway from Bowness; nearer, Gillalees Beacon is visible, upon which the Romans built a beacon to communicate between the scouting outpost fort Fanum Cocidii (Bewcastle) and the Wall fort Banna (Birdoswald).

Family intent on the trail close to Turret 41a

camp-site for walkers travelling light across the land. There are some steep descents in this next section beside a semi-field-Wall; after a dip by a hand-gate, the Path rises again beside the thick Wall which is, to all intents, a Clayton Wall minus a turf cap. Go through a further hand-gate then up the next bank to the earthen platform of **Milecastle 41**.

A substantial descent leads into the north-facing combe of **Bogle Hole**, 'the goblin's hollow', its name betraying local superstitions about the haunt of evil little folk. A final steep descent puts the Path onto the road at **Caw Gap**; cross, via the facing kissing-gates, to embark upon a superb section of consolidated Wall. Pass the outline of **Turret 41a**, skipping over a sequence of three stiles before steeply stepping down to **Thorny Doors** (ignore the hand-gate). Here the Wall momentarily stands 14 courses high coping with the pitch of the slope. This next gently declining passage is truly delightful, consolidated Wall running alongside the wooded scarp of **Cawfields Crags**.

Thorny Doors

▶ The Wall snakes down to **Milecastle 42**, set awkwardly on a slope above Hole Gap. The natural weakness in the Whin Sill was purposefully blocked, forcing carts to plod through this steep control. To get a good view, climb to the top of the truncated peak opposite the kissing-gate; the milecastle looks jaunty, but doubtless the auxiliaries and native Brits will have used a different adjective. The north gate masonry is substantial – notice the guide-lines etched on the top surface of the stones. A great tower stood over this gateway, making this quite a landmark; it appears that the fort and milecastle towers were the 'crows' nests' of the frontier, which explains why the turrets were removed and why, indeed, current thinking has dismissed the notion of a wall-top walkway. The vallum is a striking feature all along the dip slope from Cawfields, with the Stanegate converging upon a cluster of **marching camps** above Haltwhistle Burn just to the south. Looking south see the Milecastle Inn, now named after the Milecastle 42, although it was once known as the North Jerry. A 'jerry' was a beer-house with the ale served in jugs for the navvies building the Military Road and for later travellers.

In this vicinity both Roman and later bell-pit shafts were sunk to exploit the excellent quality coal found

It is rare to wander this way and not encounter rooks, their chattering antics giving rise to the crag- and farm-name Cawfields, 'farmland frequented by rooks, crows and jackdaws'.

Milecastle 42

close to the surface. Haltwhistle lies down the valley from here. The town's proud boast is that it is the 'Centre of Britain', and the centre for the Wall it most certainly is. Some visitors have construed the name to mean a place for whistle-stop visits. Local hoteliers are not too keen on that perception; they would wish visitors to know it really means 'the wood and the meeting of streams' – which is not half as much fun.

The Path slips via hand-gates to **Cawfields Quarry picnic site** and car park, with the very chilled waters of a quarry pond lending added sparkle to the scene. Watch out for six-foot black frogs – as frogmen frequently use the site for scuba diving training (book through National Park Rangers should you be interested!).

↦E EASTBOUND 16 The Path leaves the car park along the path beside the quarry pool, and proceeds via kissing-gates to Hole Gap. Bear up left by Milecastle 42; the lower section of the consolidated Wall is fenced off because it is too low for stock-proofing. Ascend beside the fine stretch of Wall along the rising ridge of Cawfields Crags, stepping up above Thorny Doors via stiles. Advance by Turret 41a to cross the Caw Gap road by facing kissing-gates. The roller-coaster ridge climbs and dips beside the semi-field-Wall, by Bogle Hole and the grassy earthworks of Milecastle 41. Proceeding by hand-gates it rises to the Ordnance Survey pillar on the top of Winshields Crags, the highest point on the entire walk. Soon a further stretch of consolidated Wall is passed on the easy descent to Milecastle 40; then, by a hand-gate and later gateway, decline gently, with the impressive view of the Wall scarps to Peel, Highshield and Hotbanks Crags straight ahead.

18/15

Cawfields Quarry ⇄ Walltown Crags

The Whin Sill's final flourish, and a
rubble rigg becomes a mighty monument

Distance: 3.2 miles/5.1km

←W WESTBOUND 18 Exit Cawfields Quarry car park by the cattle-grid; across the road is a picnic area on either side of the burn. This was the site of a Roman water-mill for grinding corn. Today, amid the alder carr, the stream-side yields flowers instead of flour. Bear left and right over the Haltwhistle Burn road bridge, skipping over the wall-stile immediately on the left. Pass discreetly by the refurbished Burnhead Cottage, coming alongside a field-wall with the north ditch beyond. ◄

The impressive view to Cawfields and Winshields Crags giving cause for many a backward glance. Having strode the great Whin Sill wave from Sewingshields it feels odd to be striding over level pastures, but the ridge will swell again for one last rapture.

Cross a ladder-stile, and after some 150 yards the adjacent wall staggers right to reveal two small portions of dry-stone walling. After another ladder-stile the walk approaches **Great Chesters Farm**, striding to a ladder-stile left of the farmhouse and buildings, which unfortunately encroach upon Aesica Roman fort.

The Path leaves by the western corner, with the unusual feature of double ditches apparently defending this side of the fort. The Wall exists only as a rubble rigg beside the Path, resuming as a field-wall with two ladder-stiles in quick succession to pass **Cockmount Hill**, the partially derelict farmstead named after 'the lekking ground of woodcock'. A ladder-stile puts the Path into an open pine wood, bearing right to join the line of the Wall, which here has attracted bramble in profusion. A gravel Path wends on between the birch and conifers to a ladder-stile.

Once on the far side, look right to the field gateway, which shows Wall foundations and a distinctive round milestone removed from the Military Way to serve as a gatepost! The way ahead follows the poor field-wall

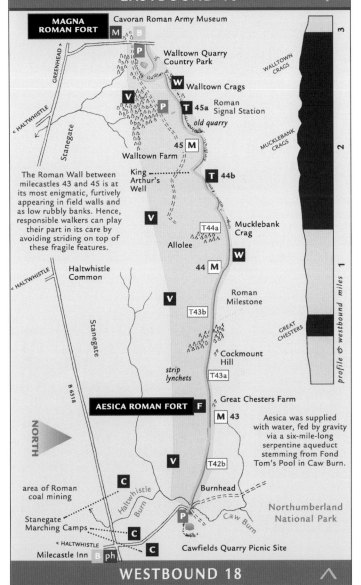

MAGNA ROMAN FORT

Cavoran Roman Army Museum

M B

P

Walltown Quarry Country Park

WALLTOWN CRAGS

< GREENHEAD >

W Walltown Crags

V

P T 45a Roman Signal Station

old quarry

< HALTWHISTLE

Stanegate

45 M

Walltown Farm

MUCKLEBANK CRAGS

King Arthur's Well

T 44b

The Roman Wall between milecastles 43 and 45 is at its most enigmatic, furtively appearing in field walls and as low rubbly banks. Hence, responsible walkers can play their part in its care by avoiding striding on top of these fragile features.

V

T44a Mucklebank Crag

Allolee

W

44 M

< HALTWHISTLE

Haltwhistle Common

Roman Milestone

V

T43b

Stanegate

GREAT CHESTERS

B 6318

Cockmount Hill

strip lynchets

T43a

AESICA ROMAN FORT F Great Chesters Farm

M 43

NORTH

Aesica was supplied with water, fed by gravity via a six-mile-long serpentine aqueduct stemming from Fond Tom's Pool in Caw Burn.

V

T42b

area of Roman coal mining

C

Burnhead

Haltwhistle Burn

Caw Burn

Northumberland National Park

Stanegate Marching Camps

C

P

< HALTWHISTLE

Milecastle Inn B ph

C

Cawfields Quarry Picnic Site

profile & westbound miles 3 2 1

AESICA FORT

The situation of the fort, only three miles from Magnis, is odd, being a later expedient implant. In purely practical terms there was a problem – a natural water supply was non-existent. Roman surveying guile was tested in bringing a head of water some six miles along a serpentine aqueduct on a slight gradient from Fond Tom's Pool, located only two miles distant in Caw Burn. A notice on the stile confirms your liberty to wander around the fort enclosure, a rudimentary plan giving a clue to the layout. Many walkers will be attracted to the central fenced arch – remains of the head-quarters building's cellar strong-room. However, one should not ignore the south-east corner gateway, where an altar attracts modern votive offerings of coins; notice, too, the crude relief of a Roman soldier holding

South gate at Aesica, the altar attracts coins and the crude relief of a soldier with shield attracts the eyes

a shield at arms length on the adjacent block. Work your way round the southern edge; in the grass bank are traces of barrack blocks. The more intriguing western walling includes the partially blocked west gate. Horses and cattle have equal liberty with walkers loafing about this arcadian site, daily challenging the survival of this precious antiquity.

Vaulted strong-room arch, headquarters building, Aesica

resting on the rubble rigg in rough undulating pasture. After a large sheep creep, with rusting corrugated iron cap, the Wall intermittently grows again beneath the ragged field-wall, though the best sections are hidden from view on the shadowed northern side and are not accessible to the Path. Cross the grassy banks of **Milecastle 43**, the ditched effect the result of stone-robbing with the in-fill cast aside.

A ladder-stile puts the path onto the first real hill element of the Nine Nicks of Thirlwall. The rubble rigg holds to the spine of the ridge. The Path, respecting the vulnerable archaeology, contours to the left, dipping into the first of the so-called Nine Nicks (or gaps), and in so doing crosses a ladder-stile. Now it leads up and over the next bank, climbing from the second gap onto **Mucklebank Crag**, the highest part of this ridge, again the path keeping off the rubble rigg. ▶

Descend to encounter the most dramatically sited turret of them all, number **44b**. One can almost sense the Roman patrol keeping their ghostly watch. The slope from here is steep, and walkers are beseeched to keep left and avoid treading on the rubble rigg and the adjacent wear marks of the all-too-hasty. Periodically tank traps

This is a superb viewpoint, and the name appropriately means the 'big hillside'. From here one can see Skiddaw Little Man and Skiddaw over the shoulder of Talkin Fell down to the south-west, Cross Fell at the head of the South Tyne valley, Gillalees Beacon to the north-west, and the great dark horizon of the Border Forests across the northern arc of the view.

Turret 44b looking over Walltown Gap

are positioned hereabouts to gently guide walkers onto a new, more appropriate grassy line.

Flags guide to a ladder-stile in Walltown Gap, near the so-called **King Arthur's Well**. The spring is associated with the baptism of King Edwin, who ruled the Deira division of the kingdom of Northumbria in the early seventh century. This ceremony marked his conversion to Christianity in AD627 by the monk Paulinus.

The Wall has mesmerised romantics from many a century, so it is little wonder that King Arthur has found his place in this setting. Conversations with locals suggest they take it for granted that he was here, or why else would Paulinus choose this spot?

Cross the farm track onto the following ridge above **Walltown Farm**, historically the home of the Ridleys. Look back to a little knoll crowned with trees giving a pleasing subject for the camera. Striding onto the ridge and along the close-cropped turf by the platform site of **Milecastle 45**, soon the rubble rigg drifts into the abyss as it comes to a rude and cruel end above Walltown Quarry. Keep left, with the single strand of barbed wire affording modest protection on a considerable cliff. Rock-climbers

Walltown Quarry

have been known to give this detached portion of the quarry their attention; notice the metal loop for attaching karabiners.

Walltown Wall

The next rise brings **Turret 45a** underfoot. A skewed angle and the fact that the Wall abuts suggest that this served as a signal station for nearby Magnis Roman fort long before the Wall was built. Having hardly seen a soul since Cawfields Quarry, the crowd that converges at this hilltop may come as some surprise – a little car park down the slope on the access road to Walltown and Allolee Farms gives the more casual visitor every encouragement to discover this splendid spot. All the more splendid is the continuing switchback course of the Wall. Cameras will be in your hands every step of the way as the Wall kinks and bobs to avoid the Whin Sill, rock outcropping perched above the wooded scarp. Spot the occasional drain at the base of the Wall and the really curious splayed stepped section where it negotiates a curved dip. Again, the Wall meets its Waterloo at the quarry edge. Follow the protective field-wall left down to a kissing-gate and the fenced path into the great bowl of the old quarry.

Hadrian's wall on Walltown Crags, snaking through Whinstone Outcrops in the rich orange light of a late autumn evening

The working life of the 40 acre quarry ended in 1978. The dense basalt, prized for more than road-building purposes, took a considerable length of the Wall and the shortfall of gaps from the Nine Nicks of Thirlwall. Regimented trees are an attempt to breathe new life into the hollow where mosses flourish on the soil-bereft floor. The pool is the happy home of mallard and, in their season, frogs hop onto the paths that lead into the car park. ◀

Walltown Quarry would be the ideal location for a festival of the Wall – maybe one day!

➤E EASTBOUND 15 Wander through the car park and by the pond. Take the central, latterly fenced path up to the south-eastern corner of the landscaped quarry enclosure, pausing *en route* to look at the hexagonal metal tubes simulating the cliff above. Turn left, rising to meet the Wall. Traverse by the outcroppings of Whin Sill in harmony with a wonderful section of consolidated Wall dipping and rising to Turret 45a, adapted from an earlier Roman signal station associated with Magnis. Keep to the undulating ridge beyond the older quarry, passing over the grassy platform of Milecastle 45, and descend into Walltown Gap. Flagstones guide, via a ladder-stile, to the foot of a very steep bank. Climb some 300 feet by the sensational Turret 44b to top Mucklebank Crag. The Path slips through a depression and over a second ridge, and goes down by a ladder-stile within the ninth of the Nine Nicks of Thirlwall. Keep off the spine of the ridge where the rubble rigg persists, contouring to a ladder-stile with a tantalisingly long view ahead of the Wall's progress on the re-emerging Whin Sill ridge of Cawfields and Winshields Crags.

From this point, to Cawfields, the ridge shrinks, though initially the Wall has more substance beneath a modified field-wall. Cross the grassy bank of Milecastle 44 and go on over undulating rough pasture to a ladder-stile. With a mature conifer plantation left, bear down on the bramble-smothered bulk of Roman Wall. The gravelled Path leads through to an open pine wood, via a ladder-stile, into the pasture in front of Cockmount Hill. Keep faith with the line of the Wall by field-walls and two ladder-stiles, drawing close to Great Chesters beside a considerable rubble rigg.

Enter the fort by its north-western corner guard-house. Traverse by the fenced strong-room arch to a ladder-stile some 20 yards right of the farm buildings. Follow on the same line by a series of ladder-stiles, passing Burnhead Cottage, then go to a wall-stile onto the road. Cross Haltwhistle Burn, going left to enter Cawfields Quarry car park.

19/14

Walltown Crags ⇄ Gilsland

Magnificent views, a romantic
ruin and the ultra-refined air of a spa

Distance: 3.9 miles/ 6.3km

◄W WESTBOUND 19 Leave the car park by the cattle-grid entrance, turning right. A leftward turn would quickly bring you to Carvoran Roman Army Museum, part of the Vindolanda Trust's superb interpretative work in the Wall arena, which brings the life and times of the Roman Wall to a wide, appreciative audience. An atmospheric and inspirational film is currently the main attraction, and there is a cafe for museum visitors.

The Path follows the road north until, slipping through the emergent line of the north ditch, it turns left over a stile, short of the cattle-grid. Ahead the westward view draws the eye into the valley leading towards Gilsland, with the vallum and north ditches apparent. Accompany the north ditch down to a ladder-stile, and note the odd mass of ground-swelling like a land-slip. Continue down the bank towards **Duffenfoot**. The lower section of the ditch is protected from farm-stock as the

MAGNA ROMAN FORT

In the field behind this former farm lie the faint earthworks, levelled by farming, of Magna Roman fort. Magna, 'the rocky place', does not fit with the logic of the Wall, though it must have come to play some significant role. It was built well before Hadrian's time, marshalling the Roman road system at the point where the southbound Maiden Way met up with the Stanegate. The fort lies some 300 yards to the south, excluded from the military zone defined by the vallum. In Hadrian's time the fort was associated with the first cohort of Hamian archers, the crack bowmen of their time brought here from Syria – very much the forerunners of the yeomen of England!

141

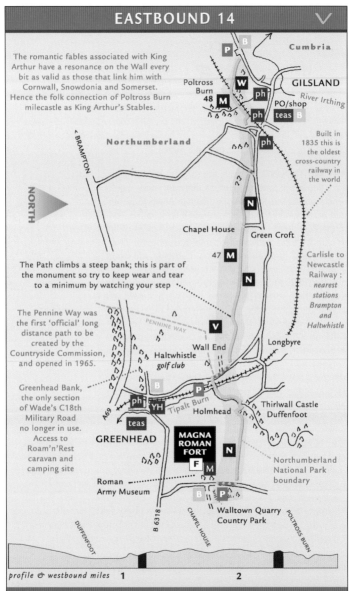

The romantic fables associated with King Arthur have a resonance on the Wall every bit as valid as those that link him with Cornwall, Snowdonia and Somerset. Hence the folk connection of Poltross Burn milecastle as King Arthur's Stables.

Cumbria

P B

GILSLAND

Poltross Burn W ph
48 M PO/shop
ph teas B

River Irthing

< BRAMPTON

Northumberland

ph

Built in 1835 this is the oldest cross-country railway in the world

NORTH

N

Chapel House Green Croft

47 M

Carlisle to Newcastle Railway : *nearest stations Brampton and Haltwhistle*

The Path climbs a steep bank; this is part of the monument so try to keep wear and tear to a minimum by watching your step

N

The Pennine Way was the first 'official' long distance path to be created by the Countryside Commission, and opened in 1965.

PENNINE WAY

V

Wall End

Longbyre

Haltwhistle *golf club*

Greenhead Bank, the only section of Wade's C18th Military Road no longer in use. Access to Roam'n'Rest caravan and camping site

B

ph YH
A69 *Tipalt Burn*

P

Holmhead

Thirlwall Castle Duffenfoot

teas

GREENHEAD

MAGNA ROMAN FORT

N

F
M

Northumberland National Park boundary

Roman Army Museum

B P

Walltown Quarry Country Park

DUFFENFOOT

B 6318

CHAPEL HOUSE

POLTROSS BURN

Thirlwall Castle

path funnels to a gate and wall-stile, with Thirlwall Castle well screened by the beech grove. The track hair-pins down to **Holmhead**. An acorn seat might appeal; however, more interesting is the stone-slated out-barn with two stone-built pillars in the facing wall, indicating the original line of the Roman Wall. On the kitchen wall in Holmhead, far-famed among guests for its breakfast feasts, an inscribed Roman stone reading 'CIVITAS DUMNON' has been inserted. This authentic graffiti relates to Dumnoni slaves, Celts from the Exeter area of Devon, who would have been marched up to repair the Wall close to Magna; it was unusual for natives to work in their own land. The Romans were masters of the divide and rule principle, bringing a 'united nations' of men from all around their empire to do service in a foreign land.

Cross the footbridge over **Tipalt Burn** to the cluster of cottages known as Duffen or Doughan Foot; where Duffen Head was is unclear. Presumably there have been dwellings here for a long time, taking shelter and serving the needs of the masters of **Thirlwall Castle**, which stands

Greenhead Millennium Green

an imposing romantic ruin above. The name Thirlwall means 'hole in the Wall'. Did the castle builders exploit a hole or create one by using the available stones for their magnificent tower? To the casual eye, every last stone looks Roman; and there were probably plenty of stones available, as in the 1600s most Roman structures existed to somewhere near their original height. The medieval barons, the de Thirlwalls, lived in troubled times, but were clever enough to plunder more than they ceded, hence the tale of the Golden Table guarded by a Black Dwarf. Reputedly he gave Scottish raiders the slip by throwing the table and himself down a well! Make the short climb to ponder this splendid site; its restoration is the largest of its type undertaken by the Northumberland National Park Authority.

The Path goes through the hand-gate and follows the green lane beside the stream to cross the footbridge over Pow Charney Burn at its waters-meet with Tipalt Burn – 'pow' means a 'sluggish stream'. To the left a footpath passage leads tight by the railway into Greenhead. The village has a youth hostel, hotel and cafe. Situated on the Military Road (the advent of the A69 relieving it of the heaviest traffic), the old Greenhead Bank road is a notorious accident black spot. Fanciful stories give Greenhead as Saint Patrick's birth-place; these deserve little currency. The streamside green, opposite the church, opened by the famous footballer Jackie Charlton is, however, a more tangible delight.

The Path crosses the railway by facing kissing-gates; the 'stop, look, listen' warning deserves respect! The little terrace of red-brick cottages was built in 1907 for the colliery captains of Barn Colliery, while the colliers' terraces are at nearby Longbyre. ▶ Pass the abutment-like raised Wall foundation stones, and note the tall barn ahead – not the original source of the name Longbyre.

Turn up left, via steps to a ladder-stile. Ascend the pasture to a ladder-stile next to Wall End house; note the old sheep dip to the left. Traverse the field to a ladder-stile and plank bridge over the small stream that defined part

Meeting the road the Pennine Way, opened in 1967, heads off up the bank ahead beside Haltwhistle Golf Course, while the Wall Trail goes right along the verge.

Longbyre Wall

of the north ditch. Ascend the bank, witnessing the rebirth of a substantial north ditch. Avoid treading on the rubble rigg beside the field-wall. Soon come alongside a thorn bush and disfigured section of the north bank of the north ditch; this is an active badger sett. All along this section the ridge of the north ditch is distinctly higher than normal. Here the excavation material, normally dispersed by the Romans, was heaped up and has, remarkably, remained intact. After the next ladder-stile a mass of small stones has been wantonly thrown into the north ditch.

Approaching Chapel House Farm the north ditch dissolves, and after a light stile the Path crosses a gated footbridge; again a stream renders the north ditch superfluous. Pass on by a low ladder-stile and gates through a garden filled with gnomes – is this where the Black Dwarf of Thirlwall can be found? The name **Chapel House** indicates that the farm was once a Primitive Methodist meeting house. Follow the farm lane right by **Green Croft**, resting plumb upon the course of the north ditch. Take the ladder-stile at the right-hand bend. Agriculture has done away with the north ditch for a while, and the path mounts a bank to a stile.

Keen frontier spotters with an eye on the map will note that hereabouts the main components of the Wall all come into their most intimate concert – Stanegate, vallum, Military Way, Wall and north ditch. Bearing off the wall-end descend the bank to a muddy passage with a gravel apron leading to a ladder-stile onto the minor road between Gap Farm and a bungalow. ◄

The name 'gap' for the farm is appropriate, for in this vicinity the Path crosses over the Tyne Gap and the watershed of England, though the name probably refers to a gap in the old Wall. The Path is now set irrevocably on course for the Solway. All the waters henceforward drain into the Eden.

Go right then swiftly left at a kissing-gate, slipping through the farmhouse garden; watch the strawberries as you step over a ladder-stile and ascend the pasture bank to enter and follow, for the one and only time, the floor of the north ditch. A recessed stile deports into the yard where a Roman soldier's shield is displayed. This the home of 'Jefficus', who lives and breathes the Roman experience in legionary costume. His demonstrations, which are hugely educational and entertaining, are enjoyed by young and old alike. Cross the road, by facing

North ditch looking west from near Chapel House

stiles, into a paddock where gravel strips remain from the September sheep auction mart, last held in 1989.

Back on track. Cross a stile, go right, and the north ditch falls away towards the Poltross Burn. A kissing-gate puts the Path at the end of the Station Hotel yard beside a village heritage board. Follow the confined path, and a right turn leads beneath the railway down into the village. However, descend to the concrete steps and the footbridge spanning **Poltross Burn**; the tall, arched railway bridge is striking. Ascend the corresponding steps, witnessing the re-emergence of the Wall up the steep bank to link into **Milecastle 48**, once fabled as King Arthur's Stables. Though damaged during the construction of the railway, enough has been salvaged to show a near complete picture of the internal features of a large milecastle, arguably the best on the entire frontier system. One can understand how in folk tradition these were thought to be ancient stables – the barrack blocks being large enough

GILSLAND

In its heyday Gilsland was a spa resort to rival Bath and Harrogate, with the railways bringing large numbers to partake of the sulphur spring. The old Spa Well was built in 1740, its development hindered until then by the lawless nature of the area. It is located just below the Gilsland Spa Hotel, prominently sited to the north of the village overlooking the Irthing gorge. This hotel was built in 1859 following a fire that destroyed its predecessor, the Shaws Hotel. The present well-patronised hotel belongs to the North Eastern Co-operative Society. Of the many who have known and appreciated these waters – in spite of the fact that sulphur springs smell like rotten eggs – perhaps Sir Walter Scott was the most famous. Sir Walter came here in 1797, stayed at Wardrew House and met his future bride, whom he proposed to at the Popping Stone in the gorge. The setting may have had many similarly romantic moments after this time. An analysis of local mosses has indicated that the air here is the purest in England – the perfect ambience for romance? Indeed, couples were in the habit of chipping chunks off the Popping Stone and putting them under their pillow when they became betrothed! The Romans also used the waters, and a most unusual altar was found that referred to the health of the empress.

The River Irthing is as black as pitch, not because of coal, but from peat erosion. It drains the huge mires of the 65,000 acre Spadeadam Forest, itself part of the 250 square mile Border Forests tended by the Forestry Commission. Upon the Gillalees Beacon ridge is a dry-bombing range – hence the mid-week 'treat' of low-flying jets.

to house 30 men. Of most interest, perhaps, the low steps onto an internal walkway that has been estimated to be 15 feet above ground level. The north gate was partially walled-up; see the ovens in the north-west corner.

From a kissing-gate a confined path leads to a second serious crossing of the Carlisle–Newcastle Railway. To the west, the line stretches away into the distance, but to the right, a curve brings a speeding train bearing down smartly, so it is important to 'Stop, Look, Listen'. Before descending the incline, survey the consolidated Wall crossing the pasture from the railway embankment to the sadly decrepit old vicarage. This large, square, pale-brick building has certainly fallen on hard times, its garden poached from livestock activity.

A kissing-gate puts the Path into pasture; the Path then aims diagonally to a clapper bridge over a ditch, rounds the hedge corner of the primary school then marches along flags to a kissing-gate onto the road. Immediately left is a convenient car park, of particular use for access to the Willowford Roman bridge abutment.

A footway leads down into the village passing Hall Terrace, formerly 'Mumps Ha', referred to in Sir Walter Scott's novel *Guy Mannering*. In the 17th century the proprietress was known to board brigands, and such free-booters made the village a place to be avoided. One may note that Poltross Burn and the Irthing, north from the Bridge Hotel junction, form the Northumberland border with Cumbria, hence the milecastle lies in Cumbria, as does nearly half the village. For practical purposes, it is treated as a Northumbrian community, though the suggested establishment of regional assemblies for north-west and north-east England may create ticklish problems.

Poltross Burn Milecastle 48, showing the base of steps that led to a parapet walk about the milecastle

➡E EASTBOUND 14 Leave the road to the right of the primary school, via the kissing-gate, treading a flagged path. At the corner, bear left over the clapper bridge traversing the pasture to a kissing-gate rising to cautiously crossing the railway. A confined path leads left into the enclosure containing Milecastle 48. Pass on down the steps and cross the footbridge spanning Poltross Burn entering Northumberland. The confined passage leads to the heritage board at the end of the Station Hotel car park; go right through the kissing-gate passing a cottage, then left over a stile crossing the paddock to a recessed stile. Cross the road and the subsequent recessed stile, advance within the north ditch, and where this opens angle down the slope to a ladder-stile into a garden. Follow the Path round to a hand-gate, through the small paddock to a kissing-gate onto the road. Go right, cross the ladder-stile right of the bungalow, and from a gravel strip rise up the bank ahead to follow on with the field-wall to the right. Traverse an intermediate wall by a ladder-stile *en route* to another ladder-stile into a farm lane.

Go forward, slipping through a annexed garden left after Green Croft. Proceed via hand-gates to a low ladder-stile and cross the gated footbridge. Trend left via a light stile, and follow the field-wall by a ladder-stile. As the north ditch ends, go down the slope to cross a plank footbridge with adjacent ladder-stile. Traverse the next field to a ladder-stile beyond the old railway waggon, and continue down to a ladder-stile and steps onto the road. Go right to a hand-gate on the left in front of the red brick terrace joining the Pennine Way advancing to facing kissing-gates. Cautiously cross the railway: remember 'Stop, Look, Listen'. Go over the footbridge following the streamside path to a hand-gate opposite the access to Thirlwall Castle ruins. Go right, crossing the footbridge at Duffen Foot and passing on the lane by Holmhead; the track takes a hairpin *en route* a wall-stile. Ascend the pasture with the north ditch close right crossing a ladder-stile above a swollen bank. Complete the ascent to a stile onto the road. Go right to enter the Walltown Quarry car park.

Roam on beside a classic stretch of Wall

Distance: 1.3 miles/2km

◄W **WESTBOUND 20** Go through the hand-gate beside the cattle-grid, giving access to Willowford Farm. Immediately, consolidated Wall runs beside the open

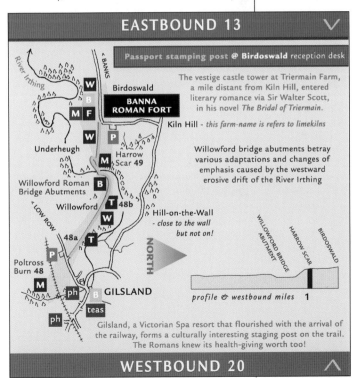

EASTBOUND 13 ⌄

*Passport stamping post @ **Birdoswald** reception desk*

Birdoswald

BANNA ROMAN FORT

The vestige castle tower at Triermain Farm, a mile distant from Kiln Hill, entered literary romance via Sir Walter Scott, in his novel *The Bridal of Triermain*.

Kiln Hill - *this farm-name is refers to limekilns*

Underheugh

Harrow Scar **49**

Willowford bridge abutments betray various adaptations and changes of emphasis caused by the westward erosive drift of the River Irthing

Willowford Roman Bridge Abutments

Willowford

48b

Hill-on-the-Wall - *close to the wall but not on!*

48a

NORTH

Poltross Burn **48**

GILSLAND

teas

profile & westbound miles **1**

WILLOWFORD BRIDGE ABUTMENT

HARROW SCAR

BIRDOSWALD

Gilsland, a Victorian Spa resort that flourished with the arrival of the railway, forms a culturally interesting staging post on the trail. The Romans knew its health-giving worth too!

WESTBOUND 20 ⌃

Consolidated Wall and farm access track within north ditch

track with Broad Wall foundation edging visible. The rather plain half-missing **Turret 48a** has a doorway on the west side of the near wall, which shows just one touch of individuality besides the Broad Wall wings. The River Irthing has gouged out a chunk of the Wall and, while the Wall resumes briefly, field-wall appears again and continues to where the farm track breaks right through the Wall line into the north ditch. The farm track runs within the north ditch, just as the path did west of Gap Farm. The Path slips through a hand-gate into a fence-confined passage tight beside the most impressive stretch of consolidated Wall up to eight courses high, with the Broad Wall foundations up to two courses high. The partial remains of **Turret 48b** spell the end of this section and require a few strides through genuine farmyard manure at the entrance to the **Willowford** Farm. Pause to look at the centurial stone (with an English Heritage plaque on the adjacent barn wall), which is interpreted as 'From the fifth cohort the century of Gellivs Philippus (built this)'. ▶ The farm-name actually is corrupted from 'Wall ford' – willows being quite uncommon along the Irthing.

Descend the flight of steps beside the Wall onto the flood plain. Hand-gates lead to a complex of Roman **bridge abutment** features. There is a flood channel and signs that the river moved during the Roman period, with the major modification of a chariot-way and tower. This tower was probably matched by a corresponding tower on the turf Wall west side, now lost to river erosion. Kissing-gates lead to the Millennium Footbridge spanning the Irthing in a charming setting, the differing bank levels elegantly accommodated in the bridge design. The rusty metalwork is actually part of the preservation process, not a design flaw; it is the same material that has been used in the 'Angel of the North' sculpture. The Path leads through a hand-gate along a flagged pathway to unite with the Underheugh access track, switching up right steeply to enter **Harrow Scar Milecastle 49**. The movement of the river has eroded the bank to such an extent that it has left a considerable wooded cliff immediately east of the milecastle.

Centurial stones were a common feature of the Wall. They were inserted every 45 feet as a form of hallmark device to confirm of the proper completion of a section of Wall under the stated centurion. Only a few have survived, as they have been attractive targets for stone robbers.

The Path does not follow the track, but keeps to the south side of the consolidated Wall via a hand-gate. As the Wall resumes notice the regular drains at its foot, with four even before the hand-gate; these are indicative of just how wet this area must have been.

The long, steady stretch of consolidated Wall is a most popular sojourn of visitors to Birdoswald, and who can blame them? Prior to the fort there are several special stones to discover, including two phallic motifs – warding off the evil eye – and two centurial stones. The first phallic occurs some 40 yards after the Wall appears to set down beneath a southern ditch; a further 30 paces on is a brown centurial stone on the top course, which states that 'Julius Primus of the VIII Cohort [of an unspecified unit] was responsible for building this legionary length'. Then, as the Wall ends, spot a protruding drain; three paces further is a second phallic, and beneath this is a

Phallic stone on wall approaching Harrow Scar

154

stone marked with a cross. A kissing-gate beside the rounded corner of the fort marks the point of entry at Birdoswald. The curved hollow is the remains of a medieval bread oven.

Birdoswald farmhouse

↦E EASTBOUND 13 Depart from Birdoswald via the hand-gate at the north-eastern corner of the fort, though one should first stand by the broken Wall-end at the road bend to admire the view towards the craggy scarps at Walltown Crags, due east. The path runs alongside the Wall within the pasture to a kissing-gate and passes over Milecastle 49. Following the open track it pitches down the bank towards Underheugh. Near the foot of the bank watch for the flagged path signed left; this contours along the base of the bank to a hand-gate through a hedge before crossing the most handsome Millennium Footbridge, erected in 1999. Bear left, and advance by kissing-gates into the Roman bridge abutment enclosure. Keep to the left of this fascinating feature following a confined path up steps by hand-gates. Cross in front of Willowford Farm entrance – this can be quite muddy. Leave the farm track, keeping to the right of the re-emerging Wall and Turret 48b, and proceed via a hand-gate and fence-confined path beside a fine stretch of consolidated Wall. At a second hand-gate re-join the farm track and advance to the cattle-grid onto the road in Gilsland.

21/12
Birdoswald ⇄ Banks

*Stone wall, turf wall, turrets and panoramic
signal station: a great welcome to Cumbria*

Distance: 2.3 miles/ 3.7km

BANNA ROMAN FORT

◄◄W **WESTBOUND 21** The Birdoswald estate, centred upon Banna Roman fort,
is a peerless example of a historic site – with an enthusiastic, caring staff providing excellent educational facilities and guiding; it is a friendly, lively place
selling local produce and using local suppliers. As Cumbria's principal Roman
Wall exhibition fort it is a flagship for the county's many Roman sites, only bet-
tered for sheer drama by Hardknott Roman Fort (Medibogdum), with its stunning
setting. Should you sense the
magic of the place, know that
you are not alone.

By bringing their Wall
onto the north side of the
Irthing gorge the Romans gave
themselves room for fast, reac-
tive movement into hostile
territory. They could have set
the Wall close to the
Stanegate, in effect closer to
the line of the
Carlisle–Newcastle railway,
and put a real obstacle in the
way of incursionaries. The
high ground westwards to
Craggle Hill mimicked the
Whin Sill, giving good vision
to north and south, which is
good news for modern walkers on the trail. You've gazed

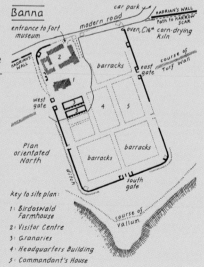

Banna

key to site plan:
1: Birdoswald Farmhouse
2: Visitor Centre
3: Granaries
4: Headquarters Building
5: Commandant's House

B **P** **T** **W** Banks **52a**

old limekiln

S

Pike Hill
Signal Station

M 52

old limekiln

Bankshead Farm
& Camping Barn

Lea Hill Farm

T Lea Hill **51b**

Craig Cottage

The footpath descending the woodland
bank to the rocky gorge beneath Combe
Crag is a spectacular and unsuspected
scenic treasure. It includes
a small Roman quarry near the top
of the heather- and pine-clad rigg.
The path leads to a handsome
footbridge spanning the Irthing and
giving access to Nether Denton.

Combe
Crag Fm

T Sandy Syke **51a**

MILLER HILL >

Combe Crag
Roman Quarry

Q

Wall Bowers

The point where the Turf
and Stone Walls converge

Nether
Denton
Church

V

M 51

Wall Burn

North of Wall Burn the Path
follows the banks of the Vallum

tw **N**

Lanerton

The best section of the turf Wall
is found in this vicinity -
it was originally topped with
a palasade fence.

High House
Farm

tw **N**

M 50

course of Roman road
to Bewcastle via
Gillalees Beacon

River Irthing

T **49b**

**Passport stamping post
@ Birdoswald** reception desk

W

NORTH ◀

F **M**
teas **B**

BANNA ROMAN FORT

Birdoswald

P

GILSLAND >

BIRDOSWALD

WALL
BURN

BANKSHEAD

PIKE HILL

profile & westbound miles   1   2

down upon Segedunum; peacefully perused the parkland setting of Chesters; marvelled at the wildness of Housesteads; and now, combining a spark from each of the above, discover the unique qualities of Roman Banna, the modern Birdoswald. It may be the sense that this consciously romanticised farm-steading only thinly disguises evidence of a long and turbulent history that makes a visit to Birdoswald special.

From the café/reception area the visitor is drawn into the barn museum, with its life-size, burly, Barbour-jacketed model of Mr Birdoswald himself, Tony Wilmott. Tony has brought his own refreshing vigour and rigour to archaeological research here at Birdoswald. People love to know that archaeology is alive and kicking – and staid exhibitions pale beside the occasional revelation. Recent study here has made giant strides in bringing forward the story of the Wall through into the Dark Ages following Roman withdrawal. Certainly there are several examples of the continuity of agricultural use of Roman structures along the Wall, the farms at Willowford and Birdoswald being clear proof. For all that, during the next 1000 and more years Saxons and others reverted to timber as the primary building material, and the Roman walls in the widest sense were used as the basis of settlements and farm estate boundaries as well as buildings. Wander around the fort area with the interpretative panels as guides.

A visit is recommended to the southern edge above the Irthing gorge, with the curling thread of the river far below and a huge sand martin colony on the nearer banks. Beyond the meadows lies Upper Denton, and the great green slopes lead the eye to the Tindale Fells overtopping the plantation on Denton Fell.

From the roadside, opposite the fort entrance, lean on the field-gate and gaze north to view the Maiden Way Roman road stretching away, crossing the Gillalees Beacon ridge to reach the outpost fort at Bewcastle (Fanum Cocidii). While half-left catch a sneak glimpse of the tall ruined peel tower of Triermain Castle, with the distinctive table-topped hill of Burnswark just discernible to the right in the hazy distance of Dumfries, the site of a Roman catapult (*onagri*) training ground. The latter was perhaps as much a psychological as a military exercise, the Romans flexing their muscles within barbarian country.

Birdoswald South Gate

Turf Wall near High House Farm

Birdoswald stood astride the first-built turf Wall, which runs invisibly across the pasture, west from the west gate – the trail will shortly unite with it. The Path leaves the environs of the farmstead via a fenced passage and kissing-gates from the rounded roadside corner of the fort wall. Slipping through an old orchard, with sapling plantings, enter open pasture. Angle right to come alongside the fence separating the path from the consolidated Wall. After a hand-gate, pass or step into **Turret 49b**. This was built with the replacement stone Wall and is therefore properly integrated, unlike all previous turrets leading to the Irthing. The Wall tapers off as its course merges with the road. Continue with the subsequent field-wall: heed the waymarking which directs up to a wall-stile on the brow, here encountering the course of the turf Wall. The Trail heads on west close to the turf Wall north ditch through a succession of kissing-gates in pasture.

Ahead are the wooded banks and knolls about Naworth Castle with Brampton Rigg prominent. Naworth, 'the new work', which was crenellated by Ranulph of Dacre in 1335, is now the seat of the Earls of Carlisle, a branch of the Dukes of Norfolk.

THE TURF WALL

English Heritage excavated Wall at the end section close to Wall Burn, revealing that the turf Wall was no hastily contrived mound. Though there was a standard Roman size to their sods, here they were not so regular, possibly because of the poor source material. When set in layers upon a firm cobbled causeway foundation, the turf made a remarkably stable structure. Unlike the vallum, which remained a substantial earthwork, it appears that the Romans disposed of much of the bulk of the turf Wall, hence only the ditch betrays its course. The only portion of the turf Wall to survive to any height is to be found closer to the High House track, back east along the trail just trodden.

Step down from the hand-gate onto the Lanerton track – presumably this farm-name means 'the farm associated with Lanercost'. Go left 70 yards, then branch right upon the track crossing both **Wall Burn**, an attractive dingle, and the emergent hollow of the vallum through the beech break. Traverse the following field, close to the site of a Stanegate fort above the wooded banks of the Irthing, with Nether Denton church prominent over to the left. Join a fence-line and flags to a kissing-gate to enter woodland. A bark-surfaced path leads through to a pair of trunks laid as guides, the origin of the term 'trunk road'.

A left turn would give access to the Combe Crag ridge and gorge, a quite sensational place to explore, with evidence of Roman quarrying as well as scenic drama, and the river running through a rock-ribbed bed.

However, the trail goes right, to the road junction. Look north along the facing road, as down the barrel of a gun, to the distant horizon of Gillalees Beacon, pinpointing the tiny mound of the Roman signal station. This was the fast-reaction warning system from Roman scouts stationed at Bewcastle for the Wall garrison at Birdoswald.

The path goes left along the minor road soon encountering **Sandy Sike Turret 51a**, which, in common

Looking east along the vallum to Wall Burn

with most turrets, was occupied only to the end of the second century AD, at which time such structures became redundant. A third of a Roman mile further along the road stands **Lea Hill Turret 51b**; you'll get no better opportunity to measure 333 double steps (Roman marching paces) and to master for yourself precisely what this distance feels like. The National Trail tries to break your rhythm by putting the path back into the roadside pasture at the top of the Gunshole Lane, beyond the sweetly renovated, traditional single-storey dwelling of Craig Cottage. Conveniently, a stile makes linking back to the trail from the turret possible. The path runs on beyond **Lea Hill Farm**, with its distinctive red byre doors and the occasional sloe bush to tempt casual harvest, and re-emerges onto the road opposite a 19th-century lime-kiln mound.

Follow the road by **Bankshead**. Here are two separate dwellings – the first was the home, from 1924, of the famous Cumbrian artists Ben and Winifred Nicholson; the second is a farm, the roadside byre commendably converted into a camping barn. A considerable proportion of these buildings is composed of re-used stone from Milecastle 52, a classic case of farming continuity, generation after generation, finding succour and shelter from this elevated location. The road is a natural ridge-way; perhaps some form of track existed here before the Romans came and adapted it for the Wall service chariot-way. It has continued to be used until today, when it forms a heritage trail for pedestrians, cars and the Hadrian's Wall Bus.

The Path is quickly ushered over a wall-stile into the adjacent pasture, and the damp ground bringing flags into use. Follow on along a natural shelf to reach a kissing-gate, with the **Pike Hill Roman Signal Station** close at hand. Degraded by road excavation in 1870, the remains of the tower rise some four feet up from the modern roadway. The tower belonged to the earlier Stanegate

Pike Hill Roman Signal Station

communication system and, being angled on a south-west/north-east axis, was askew and amalgamated awkwardly with the Wall. The doorway, facing friendly country, looks over the Irthing valley to the distant Blencathra and Skiddaw fells of northern Lakeland. The northernmost fells of the Pennines can be clearly seen, the highest and most prominent being Cold Fell with, to its right, Tarnmonath, Simmerson, Talkin Fells and Hespeck Raise, concluding with the scarp of Cardunneth Pike, collectively encircling the wild King's Forest of Geltsdale, an RSPB Nature Reserve. Across the road to the north, well-screened by trees, is an old lime-kiln, with Gothic arch, in sterling state. A narrow fenced passage now leads to the car park at **Banks Turret 52a**.

➼**E EASTBOUND 12** From the car park follow the fenced passage up to the Pike Hill Roman Signal Station, a superb viewpoint. From the adjacent kissing-gate follow the top edge of the pasture to a wall-stile exiting onto the road in passing Bankshead. A kissing-gate immediately relocates the Path back in the pasture comfort zone, for all the claustrophobia of the fence with stiles. Rejoin the road at the top of the Gunshole Lane. Follow the minor road passing the Sandy Sike turret, and at the T-junction go right by Combe Crag farmhouse, taking a left turn into the woodland behind the farm buildings. Emerge at a kissing-gate and traverse the field in the company of the vallum, dipping through the line of beeches to cross Wall Burn. Bear left with the farm track (bridleway) just 70 yards to a hand-gate in a fence. Cross a sequence of fields by kissing-gates in harmony with the north ditch of the turf Wall. At a wall-stile at the top of the rise, with Birdoswald in view ahead, bear left following the field-wall to accompany the roadside wall which becomes consolidated Roman Wall. Continue, via hand-gates, to slip through the spinney and emerge onto the road beside Birdoswald Roman fort.

22/11

Banks ⇄ Walton

The frontier becomes a green-pastured border-land all but bereft of Wall

Distance: 3.7 miles/6km

◄◄W WESTBOUND 22 Glance at **Banks Turret 52a**, noticing its thin north wall and chamfered mid-course to repel the rain, as well as the chunk of preserved masonry 'frozen' where it fell. The Path slips over a wall-stile following a gravel-and-plank-retained apron beside the roadside wall for just one field until it is deposited back onto the road. Follow the road through **Banks**, a little community that has changed less than most. Opposite Riggside glance across the field northwards to the woodland of Noble Hott. This intriguing name, akin to Hotbank, means 'the ring of trees associated with the family-name Noble'. It is thought that a Roman lime-kiln lay in here. Banks means 'up the banks from Lanercost'.

Head down the road taking the right-hand fork, and glance by a small green with a house 'resting' plumb on the line of the Wall. Dipping through the dingle, bear left and first right, rising up the lane to **Hare Hill**. Lurking behind a beech hedge is fine, upstanding portion of Wall, a veritable tower by comparison with the rest of the Wall, being the tallest section on the entire frontier. William Hutton striding along his merry way in 1802 said 'I viewed this relic with admiration…I saw no higher'. Only the lowest courses are original; the main structure was rebuilt as a romantic ruin after Hutton's time – and thank goodness it was. ◄ The lower portion of the exposed Wall was excavated and studied during spring 2004.

The Path continues up the roadway, branching left at a kissing-gate to avoid the farm entrance at Hare Hill. Flags alleviate the muddy field edge *en route* to a metal gate, and so into a lane. There is a handsome view south

The most important stone to locate here is found on the north face at head height. It is inscribed with the initials 'PP', which stands for 'Primus Pilus', and refers to the principal centurion in a legion.

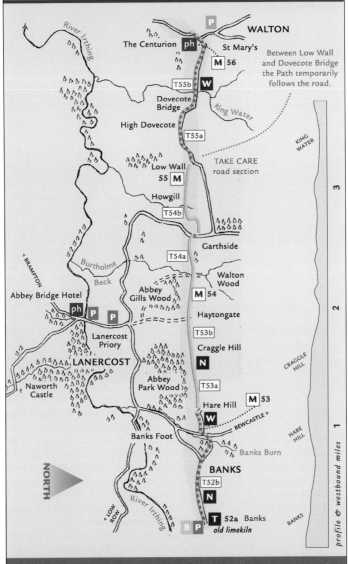

River Irthing

P

WALTON

The Centurion **ph**

St Mary's

M 56

T55b **W**

Dovecote
Bridge

King Water

High Dovecote

T55a

Between Low Wall
and Dovecote Bridge
the Path temporarily
follows the road.

Low Wall
55 **M**

TAKE CARE
road section

KING
WATER

Howgill

T54b

3

Garthside

T54a

Walton
Wood

BRAMPTON

Burtholme
Beck

Abbey
Gills Wood

M 54

Haytongate

Abbey Bridge Hotel

ph **P** **P**

T53b

Lanercost Priory

Craggle Hill

N

CRAGGLE
HILL

2

LANERCOST

Abbey
Park Wood

T53a

Naworth
Castle

Hare Hill

M 53

W

BEWCASTLE >

HARE
HILL

Banks Foot

Banks Burn

BANKS

1

NORTH ►

T52b

N

LOW
ROW

River Irthing

T **52a** Banks
B **P** *old limekiln*

BANKS

profile & westbound miles

Jefficus standing beside the Hare Hill Wall

There is a lovely rural feel to this stretch of path, reminiscent of Offa's Dyke country in the Welsh borders.

towards the Pennine fells surrounding Geltsdale. The north ditch is apparent over the field-wall. Pass on by a kissing-gate, then a step-stile tucked up beside a mature oak entering open pasture. ◄ From the next kissing-gate on Craggle Hill the Path begins to descend towards the Burtholme Beck valley, with some scant evidence of Walling at the base of the humble field-wall, a surreptitious reminder that this is still the frontier line. Craggle meant 'hill frequented by cranes', not the common Grey heron, but the Giant European crane.

A kissing-gate puts the Path onto the drive at the entrance to the tidy environs of **Haytongate**.

LANERCOST PRIORY

This is the prime moment to break from the path to visit Lanercost Priory, by taking the lane that leads directly left. Part romantic ruin, part serene parish church, it stands within a parkland setting upon the Irthing meadows. The adjacent vicarage features Edward's Tower, where King Edward I convalesced from the discomforts of dysentery for six months, along with his 200 strong court, from late in 1306. The nation was therefore governed from this spot and the monks thus impoverished!

An inverted centurial stone can be spotted on the tower. The walls of the priory were built unashamedly of plundered Wall-stone – from military device to the duty of God seems a fair exchange. The roadside wall of the priory grounds is bounded by regular Wall-stone too. The nearby Abbey Bridge is also worth visiting, a graceful bridge beside a pleasant inn – a delightful place to idle a balmy summer evening away.

The Path continues from Haytongate via a hand-gate, with hoary old oaks growing upon the line of the Wall – the fine masonry was transposed to create the new glory of Lanercost…carted down the banks at no cost! Cross the Walton Lodge track and footbridge to enter a pasture rising beside a bank with considerable mortared core Walling evident. Two kissing-gates on and the path weaves through a rank pasture of dock and rush, latterly upon stone flags, to a kissing-gate beside a holly bush and onto the road.

Go right, passing two pines, through a kissing-gate on the left. Aim quarter-left towards a solitary ash tree and kissing-gate. Descend into the damp hollow, slipping through the hedge-line below the old pine growing from the foundations of **Turret 54b** to cross a flagged bridge. Go up the bank to cross the Howgill Farm lane via facing kissing-gates. A centurial stone exists on the barn wall within the farmyard (no access). Via further kissing-gates and the invisible site of **Milecastle 55**, reach the minor road opposite Holly Bush Cottage.

The Path is obliged to follow the road all the way into Walton; plans to keep company with the Wall-line remain on hold. Passing on down by High Dovecote

Former gatehouse,
Lanercost Priory

Farm the spire of Walton church comes into view above **Dovecote Bridge**. Cross the road bridge over King Water, built in 1894, and find a clamped section of Wall in an enclosure on the right. This section of the Wall was excavated in 1983, then concealed after 20 years as it became apparent that the red sandstone could not survive permanent exposure to the elements; the condition of much of Lanercost Abbey betrays this frailty too.

Climbing into **Walton** the road makes a sharp turn beside the site of **Milecastle 56**. See opposite the distinctive white-washed 'Roman House', the cottage (however inadvertently) perpetuating the notion that the Wall was white-washed. At the road junction arrive at **The Centurion**, where beer and good locally sourced food go hand in hand for those in boots. The village name means 'farmstead on the Wall', and a brief detour right reveals a charming tree-lined green at its midst.

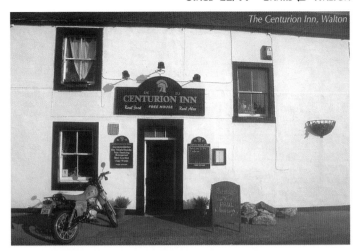
The Centurion Inn, Walton

↦E EASTBOUND 11 Follow the minor road signposted to Lanercost Abbey (*sic*) from The Centurion. The road leads down to cross Dovecote Bridge, with an earth-clamped section of Wall on the left just before the bridge. Keep to the road, winding up by High Dovecote Farm and Low Wall to reunite with the line of the Wall opposite the bungalow Holly Bush Cottage. A sequence of kissing-gates leads on, crossing the access lane to Howgill Farm, dipping into a marshy hollow with stone flags to keep the boots dry. Switch through the hedge-line and rise to a kissing-gate in the fence, then angle part-left to a kissing-gate and flags onto the minor road near Garthside.

Go right and left at a kissing-gate beside a holly bush. Flags are initially needed in this damp pasture. Proceed by a sequence of kissing-gates down to a footbridge over Burtholme Beck. Continue up the hill, crossing the access lane to Haytongate, and proceed onto Craggle Hill for a much improved all-round view, latterly in a lightly fenced lane. Keep right of Hare Hill Farm via a metal gate; flag-stones on the muddy upper field edge lead to a kissing-gate onto the road. Descend, halting briefly to inspect the eye-catching ragged Wall behind a beech hedge. At the foot of the lane go left and first right, rising through the hamlet of Banks. Just out of the community find a wall-stile right which puts the path off the road along a made-path to re-emerge at Banks Turret.

23/10

Walton ⇄ Newtown

So you like to walk undisturbed? You will here!

Distance: 2 miles/3.2km

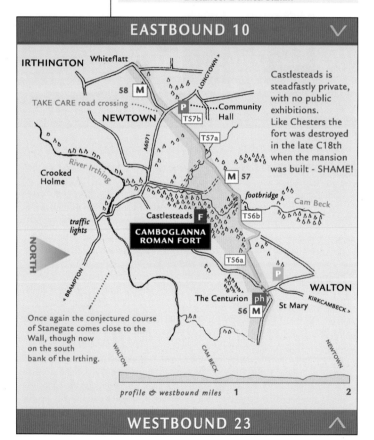

EASTBOUND 10

IRTHINGTON
Whiteflatt

58 M

TAKE CARE road crossing

NEWTOWN

LONGTOWN

P
T57b

Community Hall

T57a

River Irthing

Crooked Holme

M 57

footbridge

Cam Beck

Castlesteads F

T56b

traffic lights

CAMBOGLANNA ROMAN FORT

NORTH

T56a

P

WALTON

KIRKCAMBECK

BRAMPTON

The Centurion

56 M

ph

St Mary

Once again the conjectured course of Stanegate comes close to the Wall, though now on the south bank of the Irthing.

WALTON

CAM BECK

NEWTOWN

profile & westbound miles 1   2

Castlesteads is steadfastly private, with no public exhibitions. Like Chesters the fort was destroyed in the late C18th when the mansion was built – SHAME!

WESTBOUND 23

CAMBOGLANNA ROMAN FORT

Though not pertinent to the trail the continuing track and footpath, passing south of Sandysike Farm and outer edge of woodland via the vallum, cross parkland east of the house of Castlesteads. By this route one gets a view of the great house, built in Adam-style by a wealthy merchant from the East India Company in 1779. Castlesteads' secret walled garden rests upon Camboglanna Roman fort. The fort was unusual by its distant position, being isolated from the Wall by Cam Beck: there is positively no access for the public.

◄W **WESTBOUND 23** After a line of three bungalows the path departs from the road along a short lane accessing pasture at a kissing-gate. A green track runs beside a hedge. The footpath forks, with the trail going right.

Take the right fork to enter woodland at the cattle watering place by a flag-bridge and kissing-gate. A tidy path weaves through the grove to emerge at a kissing-gate close to Sandysike Farm. A novel collection box for St Mary's restoration fund may be found here, a pre-First World War officer's dress helmet. Go right, along the farm access lane, to reach the metalled road. Immediately go left, via the kissing-gate beside the cattle-grid, passing the entrance to Swainsteads Farm. Advance to the peaked end of the field via a gate and short muddy lane, and rejoin the line of the Wall north ditch. Go right at the next kissing-gate, only 15 yards on. Descend in the pasture with the Wall north ditch, and join a flagged path after a kissing-gate leading to the footbridge spanning Cam Beck. Just before crossing the bridge veer left to a viewing seat; the considerable curved weir is located precisely where the Roman Wall crossed the ravine, with the sizeable north ditch on the far bank. How the wall coped with this craggy crossing is difficult to imagine, but sure enough it did. Cam is derived from the Celtic meaning 'comb-shaped', as in a winding stream.

The path leads away from the wooded confines via a kissing-gate, following the invisible line of the Wall, and via further kissing-gates heading to Cambeck Hill Farm. Cross the farm track and go through the yard with the stone barn to the right, holding faith to the frontier; if wet

Footbridge over Cam Beck

conditions prevail then it will be muddy, though not gluti-nous. Keep the hedge, within what remains of the north ditch, to the left, advancing to a hand-gate and footbridge at Beck Farm. A fenced path directs right to a kissing-gate then passes round the outside of the dilapidated stone farm buildings; the slots in the walls are from the time when corn sheaves were stored for winter threshing. Return to the line of the north ditch on the westward line of the continuing hedge to a stile in a field corner, and ascend the flag-stepped bank at Heads Wood. Skirt the paling-fenced lawn to a modern adaptation of a tradi-tional stone cottage, right, angling right to a stile. Follow the hedge via stiles to emerge by the farm bungalow and buildings at **Newtown**, with the community hall close right. The open green would be a happier place without the intensity of heavy traffic that periodically punctuates the peace.

Heads Wood

⮭E EASTBOUND 10 Cross the busy A6071 Brampton to Longtown road passing between the farm and the bungalow, and wind through to a sequence of stiles advancing to Heads Wood. Skirt to the right of a paling-fenced lawn, and descend the flight of stone flags down a pronounced bank to a stile in a rank hedge. Keep the hedge close right, and at Beck Farm veer left round the stone buildings to a kissing-gate and go into a fenced passage beside a deep beck. Traverse the footbridge to a hand-gate, with the hedge right, within what is left of the north ditch, and slip through the farm buildings at Cambeck Hill. Keep straight on via kissing-gates advancing to the wooded confines of Cam Beck, and cross the footbridge; take your time – is this lovely setting. A flagged path leads to a kissing-gate into pasture, the line of the north ditch beside a fence, and to a kissing-gate into a short farm lane. Go left via a gate and along the track past the entrance to Swainsteads Farm and cross the cattle-grid. Go right, along the farm access lane to Sandysike, with a kissing-gate left, just before the farm. Follow a winding path through the woodland, exiting at a flag-bridge and kissing-gate by a cattle-drinking place. Join the open track leading to a kissing-gate and the road into Walton, only a few paces from The Centurion...now that is neat!

24/9

Newtown ⇄ Oldwall

Plane going, with no wall at all at Oldwall

Distance: 1.8 miles/2.9km

◄◄W **WESTBOUND 24** Follow the village road west from the A6071. This leads past a mix of traditional and new houses all enjoying a lovely rural outlook. In the arable farmland on the left, after the green, lies **Milecastle 58** with not a trace left behind. ◄

Proceed beyond the converging road junction at **Whiteflatt** until, as the road swings left, a kissing-gate facilitates the path's westward line with the Wall. With a fence left, follow the edge of arable land via a kissing-gate, switching sides after 25 yards at a kissing-gate in the fence: the handsome farm over to the right is **Cumrenton**.

A kissing-gate and muddy gate lead to another kissing-gate; clamber up onto the southern edge of very definite north ditch feature. The Trail now leads through pasture, with no trace of the vallum, for all that it ran close to the Wall in this field. The north ditch curves right, with mature trees embowering the path giving glimpses down the charming valley pasture, right, in the direction

Look southward to see the beech wood on Brampton Rigg and the northernmost fells of the Pennine range, surrounding Geltsdale, and the two diminutive lakes, Talkin and Tindale Tarns, both worth visiting on another occasion.

Looking east along line of Wall from the end of Oldwall Lane

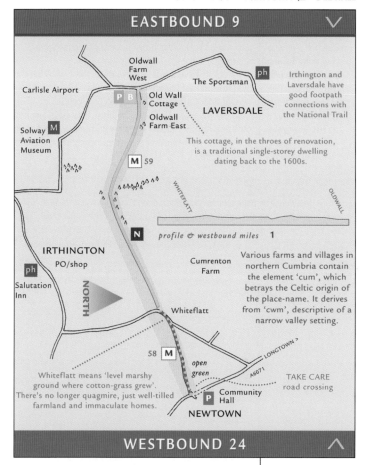

Oldwall Farm West

Carlisle Airport

The Sportsman ph

Old Wall Cottage

LAVERSDALE

Oldwall Farm East

Solway Aviation Museum M

Irthington and Laversdale have good footpath connections with the National Trail

This cottage, in the throes of renovation, is a traditional single-storey dwelling dating back to the 1600s.

M 59

WHITEFLATT

OLDWALL

profile & westbound miles 1

IRTHINGTON
PO/shop

Cumrenton Farm

Various farms and villages in northern Cumbria contain the element 'cum', which betrays the Celtic origin of the place-name. It derives from 'cwm', descriptive of a narrow valley setting.

ph
Salutation Inn

NORTH

Whiteflatt

58 M

open green

LONGTOWN >

A6071

TAKE CARE road crossing

Whiteflatt means 'level marshy ground where cotton-grass grew'. There's no longer quagmire, just well-tilled farmland and immaculate homes.

P Community Hall

NEWTOWN

of Laversdale. In this vicinity you will hear and see the occasional light aircraft lifting into the sky, the end of Carlisle Airport runway being close by. This airfield has ambitious plans to rival Newcastle...no chance!

The Trail enters the narrow, largely hedged lane at a kissing-gate; this is a drove-way only, so no wheeled

To the left, one may wander half a mile to visit the **Solway Aviation Museum**, and a comparable distance right leads to **Laversdale**, where The Sportsman promises hearty refreshment.

vehicles disturb the green sward. To the left note the dwindling scale of the Pennines, Carlisle Airport hangers and three World War II brick and pebbledash stores on the right.

Rabbits have made their mark in the hedge base as the **Oldwall East Farmhouse** comes into view. Gates lead by **Old Wall Cottage**, a fascinating 17th-century dwelling – surely built of Wall-stone rubble. The little peck of orchard, right, contains hens and a donkey – quite the good life! Two further modern bungalows lead to the road. ◀

➡E EASTBOUND 9 The line of the Wall north ditch leaves no scope to doubt the course of the path in this section. Pass on via Old Wall Lane via gates, then pasture with the ditch left. Kissing-gates serve to show the way, latterly switching sides to meet the road at Whiteflatt. Follow the street east to the main road junction by the village green.

25/8

Oldwall ⇄ Crosby-on-Eden

*A side-step to stumble upon
the Stanegate and stagger into The Stag*

Distance: 3.2 miles/5.1km

◄W **WESTBOUND 25** A kissing-gate leads into a pasture; keep the hedge to the right, and note evidence of rabbits. Do we really have to thank the Romans for introducing these little creatures to our shores? Cross the gated footbridge spanning a small ditch into arable field; path steps right continue beside the hedge. At the fence junction go through the next kissing-gate (beside a gate topped with a deterrent strand of barbed wire). The path steps right again with the hedge plainly growing in the north ditch, which is bounded to the north by a parallel hedge. Now in pasture, advance to slip through a small enclosure. Go via two kissing-gates to descend steps into

*Causeway shows
course of Roman Wall
looking east to
Bleatarn Farm*

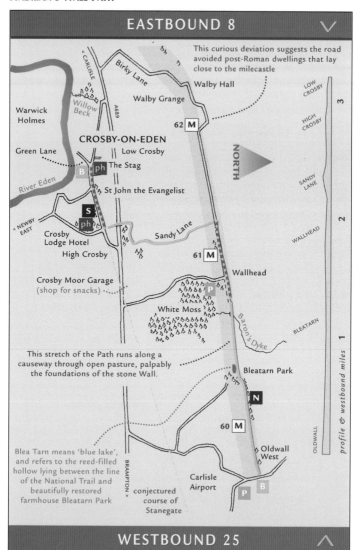

This curious deviation suggests the road avoided post-Roman dwellings that lay close to the milecastle

Birky Lane

< CARLISLE

Walby Hall

Walby Grange

Willow Beck

A689

Warwick Holmes

62 M

LOW CROSBY

HIGH CROSBY

CROSBY-ON-EDEN

Green Lane

Low Crosby

NORTH

River Eden

B ph The Stag

St John the Evangelist

SANDY LANE

< NEWBY EAST

S ph

Crosby Lodge Hotel

Sandy Lane

High Crosby

61 M

WALLHEAD

Crosby Moor Garage (shop for snacks)

Wallhead

P

White Moss

Baron's Dyke

BLEATARN

This stretch of the Path runs along a causeway through open pasture, palpably the foundations of the stone Wall.

Bleatarn Park

N

60 M

profile & westbound miles

OLDWALL

Blea Tarn means 'blue lake', and refers to the reed-filled hollow lying between the line of the National Trail and beautifully restored farmhouse Bleatarn Park

BRAMPTON >

Oldwall West

Carlisle Airport

conjectured course of Stanegate

P B

the farm lane; go left 15 yards to a kissing-gate into another small enclosure and exit after 30 yards. Enter a pasture via two kissing-gates separated by steps.

Walk along bank above the reed- and bullrush-filled Blea Tarn – the name means 'blue pool', and in the local vernacular is pronounced 'blitteren'. **Bleatarn Park**, overlooking the tarn to the south, has been radically and

St John the Baptist, Crosby-on-Eden

handsomely restored in recent years. The path traverses the pasture as a turf causeway, this being the base of Hadrian's Wall; maps suggest it was just the Roman Military Way, but it will have been both. At a kissing-gate enter a rough patch, and the path joins the concrete roadway (access to Highfieldmoor Farm) linking to the minor road at **Wallhead**.

Head west from the road corner at Wallhead Farm. Beyond the second redundant farmyard find **Sandy Lane**, a green lane signed left. The lane heads south from the Wall zone. At a lone pine get a glimpse west to Walby Grange, situated on the Wall; the name reflects 10th-century Danish settlement. Sandy Lane snakes towards the A689, but is guided right, at a stile, into a lane beside the coppice to a kissing-gate. Turn left to cross the farm-bridge over the busy highway. Avoid entry into the farmyard at High Crosby, and take the two kissing-gates from the gangway end to the footway beside the minor road. Directly opposite a wooded hollow was the course of the Stanegate. Go right following the footway into **Low Crosby**. Crosby Lodge welcomes walkers for coffee/tea in the walled garden.

→E EASTBOUND 8 Pass on the footway beyond the parish church heading to High Crosby, the height difference a matter of feet! Opposite the sign for Crosby Lodge find a kissing-gate on the left. After only some 30 yards and a further kissing-gate puts the path into a concrete gangway exiting a farm-yard. Cross the bridge over the A689.

Immediately across, go right at a kissing-gate into a lane leading, via a coppice, to a stile. Entering a further lane, go left. After winding over a gentle rise with Sandy Lane to meet a metalled lane, go right to Wallhead Farm. Keep forward along the concrete roadway; where this bears left for Highfieldmoor advance to a kissing-gate crossing Baron's Dyke. Enter a large pasture with an obvious green causeway stretching out ahead. This is the base of the Wall. Follow through beyond Blea Tarn. Weaving through small paddocks via kissing-gates, maintain the eastward journey with hedgerows in harmony with the north ditch then continue via further kissing-gates to reach the road at Oldwall.

*Going with the flow into the
heart of the great border city*

Distance: 4.3 miles/6.9km

◄W **WESTBOUND 26** Follow the village street bearing left into Green Lane, directly after **The Stag** at the little triangle by the bus shelter. This quiet, suburban side road ends at a kissing-gate. Advance along a short lane to reach the bank of the River Eden, and go right. Follow the riverbank, abundant with pink balsam and birds galore, notably gulls and ducks, but also the occasional swan. As a tributary stream interjects, the footpath is drawn right to cross a concrete bridge via a metal kissing-gate. Join an open track passing close by the gracious garden of **Eden Grove**, a handsome, single-storey porticoed lodge with bayed lawn and mature sheltering beeches alive with rooks. The track leads onto the top of the flood bank. The path curves with the river, latterly switching, through the ragged hedge, to reach a bench on the river-bank that witnesses the river flowing with vigour – as if being literally sucked by the sea. Turn back over the flood-bank, and go

*River Eden where the
path breaks off to
enter Linstock*

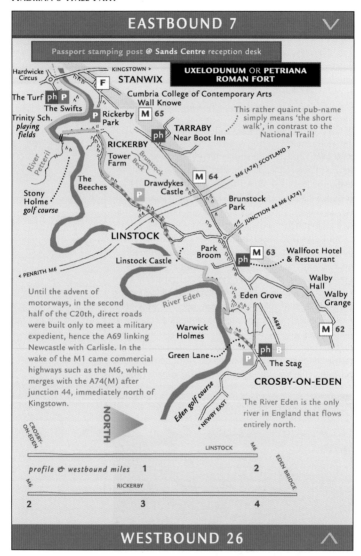

EASTBOUND 7 ∨

Passport stamping post @ **Sands Centre** reception desk

Hardwicke Circus

KINGSTOWN >

F **STANWIX**

The Turf ph P
The Swifts
Trinity Sch.
playing fields

P Rickerby Park

Cumbria College of Contemporary Arts
Wall Knowe

M 65

UXELODUNUM OR **PETRIANA ROMAN FORT**

This rather quaint pub-name simply means 'the short walk', in contrast to the National Trail!

River Petteril

RICKERBY

Tower Farm

ph **TARRABY**
Near Boot Inn

The Beeches

Brunstock Beck

Drawdykes Castle

M 64

M6 (A74) SCOTLAND >

Stony Holme
golf course

P

LINSTOCK

Brunstock Park

JUNCTION 44 M6 (A74) >

Linstock Castle

Park Broom

ph M 63

Wallfoot Hotel & Restaurant

< PENRITH M6

Walby Hall
Walby Grange

Until the advent of motorways, in the second half of the C20th, direct roads were built only to meet a military expedient, hence the A69 linking Newcastle with Carlisle. In the wake of the M1 came commercial highways such as the M6, which merges with the A74(M) after junction 44, immediately north of Kingstown.

Eden Grove

River Eden

A689

M 62

Warwick Holmes

Green Lane

P ph B

The Stag

CROSBY-ON-EDEN

NORTH

Eden golf course

< NEWBY EAST

The River Eden is the only river in England that flows entirely north.

CROSBY-ON-EDEN

profile & westbound miles 1

LINSTOCK

M6

2

EDEN BRIDGE

M6

2

RICKERBY

3

4

WESTBOUND 26 ∧

along the track to a kissing-gate into a lane. At the lane junction go left, then right at the next lane T-junction.

Directly after crossing the concrete cattle drove, close to Linstock Castle Farm, look up. The tall, ridged building beyond the farm buildings is Linstock Tower. The Tower is an adapted peel, the country home of the Bishop of Carlisle until the mid-13th century when, inexplicably, the bishop moved to Rose Castle, some eight miles south of the city. One must presume the medieval city was not an environment conducive to the dignity of this office! This peel tower can be seen again behind the next HWP sign, as the lane bends towards the housing in **Linstock** with its pleasing mix of old and new red brick. Follow the suburban lane, with Eden Nurseries right and Linstock House left. The village name means 'enclosure where flax was grown' – flax being a fibrous crop woven into linen.

A green opens, and the path follows the minor road to the main village road, turning left to cross the M6 fly-over. There can be days when the drone of motorway traffic carries back to Wallhead!

The sense of being sandwiched betwixt two military ages becomes evident should you hover a moment on the motorway bridge. Looking north one can see the next motorway flyover bridge, which lies between the course of the vallum and the Wall. Also in view is **Drawdykes Castle**, a decorative 14th-century defensive peel, a legacy from the days of Border reiving. This lies to the left,

Linstock Tower

adjacent to the site of **Milecastle 64**. Looking south, the large blue motorway sign heralds Junction 43, the junction with the Military Road (A69) constructed in the immediate aftermath of the Jacobite Rebellion in the 1750s. On the west side is a petite brick lodge with fine architectural features, only the birch thicket shielding it from the clamour of the motorway.

The road leads purposefully on and, immediately after **The Beeches**, a beautifully proportioned brick house, joins the cycle-path. **Tower Farm** actually has a tiny mock tower as a charming garden feature. Within the old estate buildings, now largely converted into the bijou homes of Rickerby Gardens, note the step-gable towers to the old stable yard. Well screened beyond is the grand Rickerby House, a late 18th-century mansion; the name is medieval and meant 'Richard's (or Richards') place'. There is a roadside telephone box at hand.

Pass the four-columned, miniature Grecian lodge with the air of a temple. Over to the right in the arable field stands a tall octagonal folly tower, with arrow slits – yet one more architectural indulgence.

The Path ends at a wide kissing-gate entering **Rickerby Park**, home of the Cumberland Show held on a Saturday in mid-July. Veer left along the metalled path with the war memorial over to the near right; the path leads directly to the Memorial Bridge. Pass through the kissing-gate and

Memorial Bridge spanning the Eden at the confluence with the River Petteril

PETRIANA ROMAN FORT

St Michael's Church, Stanwix, a prominent landmark on the far side of the river, rests on the site of the Roman Wall fort of Petriana. There is some doubt concerning the fort name, for Uxelodunum, meaning 'the high fort', is also considered a possibility. Whatever its name, this was certainly a most important fort. Covering 9.3 acres, it was the largest along the Wall: it was here that the most senior officer on the Wall was stationed.

The name Stanwix means 'stone walls', alluding to the residual walls of the fort in the Dark Ages. Between AD126 and AD400 the fort accommodated up to 1000 cavalry, the largest body of cavalry anywhere in the empire. Such a complement suggests that the need for swift defence, over the western portion of the Wall, was deemed essential from the outset. Should you make the detour to explore this area don't expect to find much evidence, though there is a tiny section of the north Wall core and three chamfered blocks tucked into a brick enclosure in the far corner of the Cumbria Park Hotel car park. The rounded corner of the fort can be traced in the tall garden wall at the junction of Well Lane and Brampton Road.

over this grey-painted metal suspension bridge erected in 1922. On the far side is the waters-meet of the River Petteril – an attractive, if unexplained, name. This modest stream has flowed some 25 miles to this spot in comparison to the River Eden's 64. The Eden's greater volume is due to its wide catchment, embracing the streams flowing off Spadeadam Forest, the western slopes of the northern Pennines and the eastern Lakes, notable Ullswater.

The Path goes along the cycle-path, continuing as a green path where this veers left, tracing the edge of **Trinity School** playing fields and then **The Swifts**, a municipal nine-hole golf course.

The unprepossessing Civic Centre building, a landmark of the 20th century, lies ahead.

There are times when floodwater can consume this area and Rickerby Park, opposite; such conditions, if fleeting, are messy and leave debris strewn on the tended fairways. A short flight of steps leads by a handsome cormorant perched on a slender plinth, which commemorates the 25th anniversary of the Carlisle RSPB group.

The Sands Centre is situated on the site of the age-old cattle market – a sale ring for those stock not exchanged through reiving! Go round the left side of the building by the car park, as this gives an opportunity to inspect The Turf, a most unusual building. As you may judge from the name, the curious roof was once a grandstand surveying Carlisle Racecourse, where the last race took place just prior to World War I. The stables lay in the basement, the old stone weighing room survives in a poor state close by (minus its slates), and the large flat car park in front of the pub the became a bowling green. The path itself passes a sign heralding the beginning of the Cumbria Coastal Way before slipping through the white-tiled underpass beneath the Eden Bridge to enter Bitts Park.

➜E EASTBOUND 7 Slipping through the underpass beneath the Eden Bridge, pass below the Sands Centre and down a short flight of flag-steps to continue upstream beside The Swifts golf course. Passing along the edge of school playing fields the Path joins a cycle-path leading to a metal suspension bridge. Cross the bridge, and from the kissing-gate bear half-right along the metalled path, advancing to the road at its cattle-grid entry into Rickerby Park. Slip through the adjacent bike-accommodating kissing-gate to follow the cycle-path beside the road and the grounds of Rickerby House. Rejoining the road at The Beeches, continue eastward, one's attention drawn to the impending motorway. The northern Pennines form the low, distant backdrop down as far as Cross Fell, the highest point on the range.

The Trail sweeps over the flyover, taking the first right on the open green; follow this village side-road, and at the left-hand bend head on down the farm lane. This leads to a lane T-junction, where you go left, and at a second T-junction go right. Pass through the kissing-gate and along a track, crossing over the flood-bank to reach a bench. Bear left, then slip left onto the flood-bank. Follow this to join the open track passing Eden Grove. On approaching an open stream bear right, and cross a concrete bridge with its green metal kissing-gate. Keep right, holding to the stream then riverbank, until you pass under a pylon line. The Path is directed left onto a lane with kissing-gate then into the suburban Green Lane to enter Crosby-on-Eden.

*Take the low road from
the castle with its guard on the Eden*

Distance: 3.1 miles/5km

◄◄W **WESTBOUND 27** The path leads along the broad
metalled way in **Bitts Park**. A walk along this tree-lined
municipal walkway with attendant well-tended shrub-
beries is quite bracing – a chance to lengthen the stride as
you hasten to find the countryside again, foot in boot
with the Cumbria Coastal Way. Hadrian's Wall, however
invisible today, was here too; the big clue is found just
short of the Sheepmount Bridge spanning the River
Caldew. Dip off the roadway right, towards the river,
where there is an unheralded a collection of 97 Roman
bridge stones (my count!) dredged from the river. The
Roman bridge spanned from Milecastle 66, perched on
the Edenholme cricket ground opposite.

With your mind refocused on the lost frontier, backtrack and cross the bridge to enter the **Sheepmount** sports
fields, with its modestly impressive athletics track. These
meadows are the old **Willow Holme**, split in two by the
railway embankment. Go right, through the car park beside the confluence of the Caldew with the Eden. I spotted
a solitary cormorant at the waters-meet, so for all the bland-
ness of the setting, you never know what you might see. ►

Now upon a grassy trod beside the willow- and
alder-fringed river, the route sweeps under the two
concrete railway bridges carrying the West Coast main
line to Glasgow. It then goes down beside unruly semi-
waste and part-active industrial land: during this section
the air can be rent with the odour of sewerage. The large
brick structures are all that remains of the **coal-powered
power station** dismantled in 1982; a mobile gas delivery
business operates now operates from this site.

The Caldew has its
source on the high
south slopes of
Skiddaw and may be
traced upon the
Cumbria Way; this
stunningly beautiful
walk extends down
through the Lake
District to Ulverston.

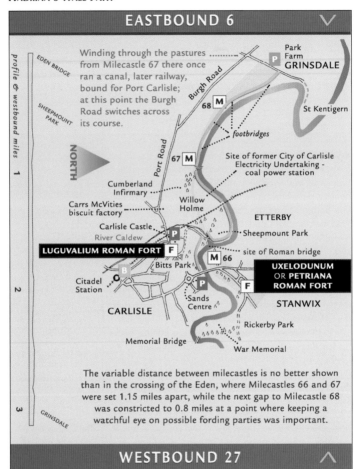

Winding through the pastures ....
from Milecastle 67 there once
ran a canal, later railway,
bound for Port Carlisle;
at this point the Burgh
Road switches across
its course.

EDEN BRIDGE

SHEEPMOUNT PARK

Park Farm
GRINSDALE

Burgh Road

68 M

St Kentigern

footbridges

Port Road

67 M

Site of former City of Carlisle
Electricity Undertaking -
coal power station

NORTH

Cumberland
Infirmary

Willow
Holme

Carrs McVities
biscuit factory

ETTERBY

Carlisle Castle
River Caldew

Sheepmount Park

LUGUVALIUM ROMAN FORT F

site of Roman bridge

B

M 66

UXELODUNUM
OR PETRIANA
ROMAN FORT

Bitts Park

Citadel
Station

Sands
Centre

F

STANWIX

CARLISLE

Rickerby Park

Memorial Bridge

War Memorial

The variable distance between milecastles is no better shown
than in the crossing of the Eden, where Milecastles 66 and 67
were set 1.15 miles apart, while the next gap to Milecastle 68
was constricted to 0.8 miles at a point where keeping a
watchful eye on possible fording parties was important.

profile & westbound miles

1

2

3

GRINSDALE

Cross Rattlingstones Beck at the site of the old bone
mill, noting the mill's skeletal remains. The river tumbles
gently on a gravel bed, passing the defunct and silted
power station outflow. Railings lead the path under an
old railway arch to rise by wooden steps: this was the last

CARLISLE (Roman Luguvalium)

While strolling through Bitts Park there are two landmark features worth perusing, firstly the Hardwicke Circus 'Peace Garden' dedicated in 1986. Being sited at the hub of the busiest roundabout in the city makes it anything but peaceful. However, pedestrians may pause amid the hubbub and read two thought-provoking plaques. One is dedicated to the Peace Garden itself, with a quote from Martin Luther King 'We must either learn to live together as brothers or we are going to perish together as fools.' The second, strikingly set against the gross 1960s architecture of the Civic Centre, is found on the monument of James Creighton, and displays this late Victorian mayor's citation on the honourable cause of service to the community.

The second landmark is in Bitts Park itself – an imperious monument to Queen Victoria. Newcastle-upon-Tyne was largely the product of the British Empire, Carlisle far less so; nonetheless, this monument exhibits the sense of civic pride felt during her reign and illustrates her place at the helm of an empire that was even larger than the limitless bounds of Roman rule. The big difference? The British Empire lasted perhaps a third of the time and allowed some semblance of self-rule to its constituent nations.

The massive walls of Carlisle Castle tower over the main walkway through Bitts Park, and only the most ardent hiker will pound on without giving the

Carlisle Castle from outside BBC Radio Cumbria

Bitts Park R Stones

castle and the historic city the benefit of a few hours' exploration. Known as both the Great Border City and The 2000 Year Old City, Carlisle stands on a battle line. It has faced the slings and arrows of a long, turbulent relationship with the land we now know as Scotland. Indeed, during the 10th and 11th centuries Carlisle and the country down to the Eamont lay in Scottish hands, and was wrested back by Rufus only in 1092.

After the Romans, there followed six centuries with scant record, though it is plain that Carlisle continued. It is even said that this was the seat of 'Coel Hen', the Old King Cole of nursery rhyme fame, the earliest ruler of the British kingdom of Rheged. In the seventh century, Rheged was taken over by the Christian Angles of Northumbria. They founded a monastery to St Cuthbert which came under the Diocese of Durham until the foundation of the Carlisle Diocese in 1133. In the ninth century, probably Carlisle's blackest hour, the Danes sacked the largely timber-built city, the destruction made complete with fire.

Turning thoughts back to Roman times…in their quick movement up country the Romans established York (Eboricum) as their legionary base. The north of the province, to and beyond the Wall, therefore came under its jurisdiction. Yet in forging their military roads the Romans soon saw the importance of holding an east–west line in the neck between the Tyne and the Solway by constructing the Stanegate (stone road) from Corstopitum (Corbridge) to Luguvalium (Carlisle). The Romans were adept at negotiating with the natives; so for all their lack of a map, they soon learnt the 'lie of the land' based on local knowledge. They often adapted existing track-ways, though some of their routes, such as the Stanegate, must have been original.

Carlisle Castle rests on part of the city's second Roman fort, Luguvalium. Recent excavation to create the Millennium Gallery and underpass beneath Castleway between the castle and Tullie House Museum unearthed considerable evidence, including a hoard of armour – though it grieves me to report that much stonework seems to have been 'mislaid'! The relationship of Petriana and Luguvalium is not properly understood, though the latter seems to have had more civil functions.

Bandstand in the lively City Centre scene

bridging point built for the Border Union Railway. Although it has been firmly fenced off, locals, particularly anglers, have breached the railings and turned it into a regular trans-river thoroughfare. And who can blame them? The bridge is sturdy, if bereft of parapets.

The Path continues above the riverbank by birch and alder scrub where once ran a series of railway sidings. The route is now precisely upon the course of the Roman stone Wall – can you visualise it? Pass the site of **Milecastle 67** – there is no clue on the ground. The Path

The portcullis Carlisle Castle

CARLISLE (Roman Luguvalium)

Approach Carlisle Castle via the gatehouse and portcullis; this is now the headquarters of the King's Own Border Regiment. Enter the castle through the English Heritage reception area/shop and take a orderly tour of the keep. Of all the sensations, the chill of the dungeons will linger longest. It was here, in the rout after the Jacobite Rebellion, that the followers of Bonnie Prince Charlie were shackled before being hanged by the Duke of Cumberland on behalf of the King. 'Ye tak the high road and I'll tak the low road, and I'll be in Scotland before ye': this emotional Scottish ballad composed after the Rebellion refers to Highlanders who died in Carlisle Castle. Their spirits travelled underground (the 'low road') back to their clan homes faster than did the few who were released and returned overland.

In 1568 Mary Queen of Scots was held in detention here. Her diary documents the first recorded mention of the game of football, when some of her entourage and local lads kicked a bladder ball – Carlisle United 1, Queen of the North 0!

Carlisle Castle

Walk down the steps and through the passage below Castleway laced with artefacts indicative of the city's history: from the curse of the Bishop of Glasgow, with all the Border reiving names, to the boots of Jimmy Glass, the 'on-loan' goal-keeper who scored a goal in injury time and thus saved Carlisle United from being relegated from the Football League in 1999.

Climb the steps at the other end and enter Tullie House Museum for a feast of heritage, culture and food, all located in the modern expansion of the original house, the oldest domestic dwelling in the city. Take time to explore within, as the exhibits reveal the fascinating background to this area

Carlisle Cathedral

of Cumbria. Walk into the garden to view a sunken native shrine – one must presume it was located close to, but not within, the Roman fort. Wander right into Abbey Street and through the Abbey Gatehouse to enter the Cathedral Close, a remarkably peaceful haven.

The Cathedral is a gracious, inspirational monument to the genius of ecclesiastical architecture. Its history is fascinating, being as much influenced by its time under Scottish ownership as during its later medieval English period. Take time to examine its many fine features including the beautiful, highly colourful nave ceiling, its diverse collection of Green Men, its stained-glass windows and treasury dedicated to Willie Whitelaw, the much-revered MP for Penrith and the Borders. To round off your visit The Fratry, the former Chapter House under-croft, now a popular restaurant and tea-room, will doubtless hold great appeal. A 'Roman menu' is available.

Old Town Hall

Having left the Cathedral visit the pedestrianised Market Square, probably a market in Roman times too. Note the Guildhall Museum, a unique survival from the medieval city. The neighbouring Old Town Hall (Tourist Information Centre) is an eye-catching building. The square in front of these buildings is frequently a scene of cultural activity, complete with bandstand and buskers. Wander along English Street to admire the twin barrel towers of The Citadel (a Victorian replacement of city's late medieval bastion south gate, built for Henry VIII by Stephan von Haschenperg in 1541) and the fine Citadel Railway Station, built in Tudor style in 1847. Backtrack via Castle Street to regain the route.

Citadel Station

goes through a kissing-gate and descends wooden steps to the footbridge spanning the less than salubrious Knockupworth Gill, while upstream Knockupworth Hall is in every way salubrious. Rising beyond, emerge from a short fenced passage at a kissing-gate and note the solitary city boundary marker stone. ▶

Of more moment and greater impact is the veritable forest of pylons carrying electricity lines across the river. Worse than these is the prospect of Carlisle's new north-western by-pass, destined to sweep through here! So let's enjoy the relative peace while we can.

After another kissing-gate, the path descends a flight of flag-steps to cross a further footbridge, with access to a riverbank bench; there is a view down to cottages at Grinsdale and back upstream to the Cumberland Infirmary backed by the Pennines. The rising path crosses the site of **Milecastle 68** in the mature pine spinney. The Path undulates within the wooded edge above the river, and a steadier step is required. On emerging at a kissing-gate into pasture keep the wooded bank to the right. Advance to a footbridge spanning a pond-like stream, then follow the fence to the kissing-gate onto the road. It is most unfortunate, or even tantamount to negligence, that the new bank flanking this footpath, created during the development of the housing estate, obliterated the Wall north ditch.

This is the tiny village of **Grinsdale**, whose name derives from 'Grimnir's valley'. It is all too easy to plough on upon the trail and ignore **St Kentigern's Church** (alternative name St Mungo), a haven of peace. You may have noticed it on your approach, secreted in a spinney to the north above the river bend. A green lane leads from the head of the street to its embowered churchyard. The charming church, built in 1740, has the most Arcadian feel.

The 1972 OS Hadrian's Wall map suggests evidence of the vallum in the field, though to distinguish it from the ridge-and-furrow is difficult. Its existence is validated by the Vallum House Hotel, located in nearby Burgh Road.

↠E EASTBOUND 6 Leave the village street at the southern end via a kissing-gate just after the entrance to the new housing estate. Advance to cross a footbridge and bear slightly right, keeping the wooded bank to the left within a pasture. Be aware that the footpath follows precisely the ancient line of the Roman stone Wall, the self-same structure that graces the Whin Sill. However, instead of the hard grey limestone, here it was built in softer red sandstone, thus this Wall-stone offered poor pickings for new buildings down the ages.

A kissing-gate puts the path in the confines of the steep wooded riverbank, and a steadier step is required. The gravel Trail opens out within a pine spinney, the former site of Milecastle 68, and descends on stone flags to a footbridge. A brief diversion left gives access to a bench on the riverbank (just occasionally consumed by flood). Ascend the wooden steps to a kissing-gate into pasture, the near right hedge-line surviving from the old railway to Port Carlisle. Follow the field edge beside the wooded bank, dipping gently via stone flags to another foot-bridge; the opposing wooden retainer steps are stamina-sapping. On reaching the kissing-gate, enter pasture with an army of power-line pylons backed by industrial estates and Belle Vue, the first of Carlisle's western suburbs.

Pass an old metal ladder-stile – the field boundary it crossed is long gone! Nearing the pointed corner of the field pass through the kissing-gate confining the path to this corner; the path now dips to a footbridge over Knockupworthy Gill, which prosaically means 'enclosure in an oak-filled stream'. A fine flight of stone steps climbs beyond to an area of alder car and birch. Next the path declines via wooden planks beneath the old railway bridge and by a short section of railings, then continues on beside the old power station with its industrial semi-waste. Keep to the riverside path under the two railway bridges and proceed on round the river bend into the long car park beside the Sheepmount Stadium. Cross the Caldew bridge onto the metalled drive in Bitts Park. With an eye for the invisible Wall, make an early diversion off the roadway half-left to inspect the dredged collection of Roman bridge stones, then continue below the castle walls to slip through the Eden bridge underpass.

28/5

Grinsdale ⇄ Beaumont

*Stride by quiet pastures
and wooded banks above the Eden*

Distance: 1.9 miles/3km

◄W **WESTBOUND 28** The footpath departs from Grinsdale village street by a newly aligned footpath avoiding the busy yard of **Park Farm**. It continues less

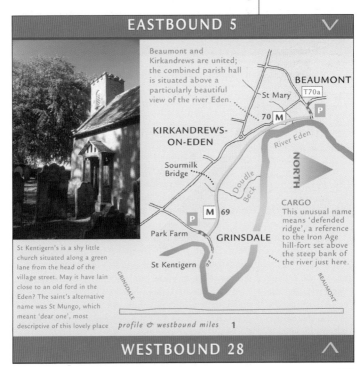

EASTBOUND 5   ∨

Beaumont and Kirkandrews are united; the combined parish hall is situated above a particularly beautiful view of the river Eden.

BEAUMONT
St Mary   T70a
P
70 M

KIRKANDREWS-ON-EDEN

River Eden

Sourmilk Bridge

Doudle Beck

NORTH

P M 69

Park Farm   **GRINSDALE**

St Kentigern

CARGO
This unusual name means 'defended ridge', a reference to the Iron Age hill-fort set above the steep bank of the river just here.

St Kentigern's is a shy little church situated along a green lane from the head of the village street. May it have lain close to an old ford in the Eden? The saint's alternative name was St Mungo, which meant 'dear one', most descriptive of this lovely place

GRINSDALE

BEAUMONT

profile & westbound miles **1**

WESTBOUND 28   ∧

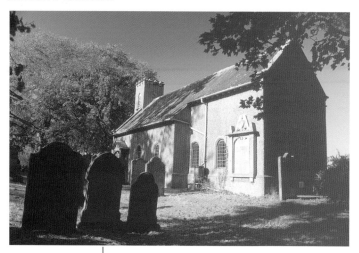

St Kentigern's, Grinsdale

intrusively via stiles to the side of the barn entering the pasture beyond. The obvious open track leads away and up a shallow bank lined with mature trees and thus rejoins the line of the Wall, heading for a gate. Keep the hedge to the left in a pasture leading to the **Sourmilk Bridge** footbridge; a stile and hand-gate with stone flag-footing make this an unusual structure, the walling allowing watering access for stock from either side. Continue with the hedge to the left and, as the field funnels, cross the stile in the fence to the right of the lane entrance gate. Keep the triple-fence close right in a pasture along the brink of an ancient flood-plain bank. Before the end of the field a double stile negotiates the fence. Ducking left under an ash tree the path wanders along the top of the bank beside a laid hedge, some 30 feet above the meadow level. Go through a wooden gate – watch your step, there is a foot-board. Descend the grassy bank within this duck enclosure complete with pond, hut and an ever-present gaggle of the raucous ducks and drakes to entertain. ◄

Locally 'duck wine' was a derogatory term for drinking water. Trail-walkers may be feeling the distance and wishing that a watering-hole was closer. The Greyhound and village post office at Burgh are still 2.5 miles/4km away.

Cross the stile into a lane, jinking slightly left into the gravelled lane ahead, below the continuing partially wooded bank. A left turn would lead into **Kirkandrews-on-Eden**; the Path therefore makes only the most fleeting connection. St Andrew's Church was demolished in the late 19th century, and the vicarage and churchyard tombs are testimony to the village's merger with Beaumont. The community is not without charm, though walkers will get no taste of it if they hold religiously to the trail.

The lane runs on beside a stream rather smothered in brightly coloured balsam growth, advances to a kissing-gate and enters a potentially damp riverside meadow exposed to winter flooding. Problems are ameliorated by a generous line of stone-flag stepping stones. One of the concerns in laying such stones is that, over the course of years, they will become so well bedded in that walkers may think them some residual part of the Roman stone Wall.

Ascend the grass bank, and at the top meet a clear footpath joining from a stile out of the adjacent recreation field containing the timber-built Beaumont Parish Hall. Now once more precisely following the Roman stone Wall, advance with the fence left, along the top of the bank, with two houses having delightful views of the Eden.

River Eden from Kirkandrews-on-Eden

Gazing upstream from this slightly elevated stance, there is a majestic view above the distant wooded bend, bringing the river back to Grinsdale. Unseen is an Iron Age hill-fort responsible for giving the little village of Cargo, on the far side of the river, its name – meaning 'the defended ridge'. Cross a stile where three footpaths are signed – the Grinsdale path refers to the one running down the bank to accompany the river upstream, and is useful to make a neat circular walk. Now confined by a hedge at the top of the wooded riverbank, advance by a distinctly Victorian brick house with formal garden to a stile by a holly bush. Entering the field proceed for some 200 yards, and the path is guided right, down a flight of steps, to the river's edge. This stretch of path is also exposed to flooding, particularly when the spring high tide coincides with heavy rainfall or snow-melt on the high Pennines and Ullswater fells. The path swings left to cross a footbridge spanning Monkhill Beck, and slips through a thicket to rise by steps and path-retaining boards through a most intriguing section known as The Heugh.

The Path has had to be diverted into the top bank pasture due to the collapse of the steep bank: the

St Mary's, Beaumont

footbridge runs not over a watercourse but a dangerous land-slip! Just before of the kissing-gate onto the road, notice the old anglers' path which winds down the bank to the ancient St Ann's Well; but there is nothing to see, so don't divert from the waymarked route. The Path now enters **Beaumont**, a village of hamlet proportions, hence its marriage with Kirkandrews. The village developed here because the site lay close to an age-old ford used by cattle drovers, who accessed the Cargo shore above the high-tide point; hence the pub at nearby Monkhill called The Drovers Arms. There is also a sail-less windmill.

When I walked this way some dozen years ago, there stood a distinguished little barn on the left, after the first stone-built hovel with its pleasing arches. It was a clay-dabbin, constructed from a series of wooden crucks, rising from ground to the roof ridge with red clay and straw walls. Sadly it is no longer there. Fortunately there are still a few examples of such vernacular buildings in the area; Burgh has an important collection of tall farm barns unique to the Solway plain.

Pass up by the telephone kiosk; in the midst of the tri-angular green is a bench surrounding a tree. It records the evidently momentous visit of the Mayor of Carlisle in 1991. Looking down upon the green from a strategic mound is the late 12th-century parish church of St Mary, the chancel windows prominent from this aspect. One should make a visit, the lovely porch leading into a charming interior. The paucity of Roman stonework in the area is relieved by its presence in this beautiful little Norman place of worship.

That the location offers far ranging views is signifi-cant – the village-name (meaning 'beautiful hill') is a reference to the extensive and beautiful view from this spot. Similarly named is Condercum Roman fort on Benwell Hill in Newcastle, which means 'good all-round view' in Latinised Celtic; indeed, the western suburbs of Carlisle have another name of this type – Belle Vue. A stone Wall and remains of **Turret 70a** have been discov-ered here; this might suggest that an earlier Roman signal station existed on the spot.

→E EASTBOUND 5 Follow the village road north-east from the triangular green to a kissing-gate entering the wooded confines of The Heugh. Walkers should be grateful for the path works undertaken in a bid to make a safe way through a most unstable slope. A footbridge spanning a notable land-slip is the first warning of the nature of the place. The path skips up and down within an environment that is at the same time visually interesting for the walker and problematic to path-keepers.

Decline through thorn scrub to a footbridge over Monkhill Beck. The path draws close to the bank of the Eden, and this is the first occasion it is witnessed as a non-tidal river. A flight of steps invites the Path up the wooded bank into the bank-top field (occasionally cultivated). Advance to a stile by a holly bush and proceed onto a confined path, the slope below landscaped by the Victorian house adjacent. A second stile puts the path onto an open section of bank-top. Advance almost to the next stile (access to the timber Beaumont Parish Hall), slipping down the bank, left, to cross a series of stepping stones to a kissing-gate into a lane.

The lane comes to a lane junction. Bear half-left to the stile entering a duck enclosure. Climb the immediate bank to a wooden gate and follow the bank-top beside a laid hedge. On passing under a mature ash tree switch up to two stiles (watch the barbed wire on your legs). Go left, keeping the triple fence close, above the flood-plain bank overlooking the patchwork of meadows; like so much of the pasture hereabouts it is faintly ribbed with old ridge-and-furrow plough riggs. A stile puts the path into a pasture, just where a lane enters from the right. Keep the hedge to the right down to Sourmilk Bridge; the stone flags give it the look of a clapper footbridge. Continue, with the hedge close right, to a gate then keep to the cart track which leads down by a clump of trees approaching Park Farm. Look right for the stile into the narrow passage leading by the barn to a stile onto the village street in Grinsdale.

29/4

Beaumont ⇄ Dykesfield

*Hammer on to and
through Burgh – watch out Scots!*

Distance: 2.4 miles/3.9km

◄◄W **WESTBOUND 29** From the triangular green, the Cumbria Coastal Way and Hadrian's Wall Path are sign-posted north along the road signed to Sandsfield. After some 30 yards the combined paths are directed left via a white house along a lane, which after The Beeches becomes a farm lane. Where two tracks join it regains the line of the Wall.

It was an interesting evolution – as the Wall followed good ground, the adjacent Military Way continued to be the link between the emerging communities of Beaumont and Burgh. The stone was pilfered (you'll shortly see for what purpose), leaving the simple trackway with enclo-sure; this was lined with hedges, though curiously aligned slightly north of its original line. ►

The firm track gives way to grass, tractor tracks and walkers' tracks, making a triple line reminiscent of the old horse and cart days. The lane ends with just the walk-ers' trod leading to a stile into open sheep pasture. Take a glance right to see Chapelcross Power Station (scheduled for imminent closure) and Burnswark, the table-top hill near Ecclefechan; the latter is the birthplace of the promi-nent Victorian Thomas Carlyle and, as the place-name suggests, a late Roman Christian site – the hill site of a Roman practice siege camp.

Ageing trees reveal the continuing skeletal remains of the lane, their sturdy trunks aesthetically pleasing sub-jects. The path advances to a footbridge, and walkers thereby avoiding wetting their feet in the adjacent ford. Spot two sections of old rail-track poking out of the silt from the nearby Port Carlisle railway. The path bears left

As the lane rises you get a good perspective back to Beaumont. Sense the raised position of the church and therefore the site of Turret 70a. Look south towards the Caldbeck fells and Skiddaw, the northernmost portion of the Lake District National Park.

HADRIAN'S WALL PATH

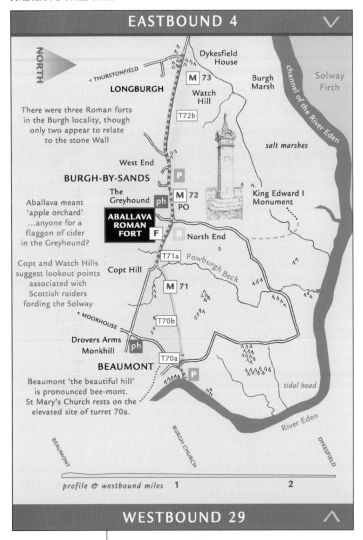

NORTH

< THURSTONFIELD

Dykesfield House

M 73

Burgh Marsh

Solway Firth

channel of the River Eden

LONGBURGH

Watch Hill

T72b

There were three Roman forts in the Burgh locality, though only two appear to relate to the stone Wall

salt marshes

West End

P

BURGH-BY-SANDS

The Greyhound

M 72

King Edward I Monument

Aballava meant 'apple orchard' ...anyone for a flaggon of cider in the Greyhound?

ph

PO

ABALLAVA ROMAN FORT

F

B North End

T71a

Powburgh Beck

Copt and Watch Hills suggest lookout points associated with Scottish raiders fording the Solway

Copt Hill

M 71

< MOORHOUSE

T70b

Drovers Arms Monkhill

ph

BEAUMONT

T70a

Beaumont 'the beautiful hill' is pronounced bee-mont. St Mary's Church rests on the elevated site of turret 70a.

P

tidal head

River Eden

BEAUMONT

BURGH CHURCH

DYKESFIELD

profile & westbound miles   1   2

Massive tree trunk on line of wall en route to Burgh

outside (but adjacent to) the hedged lane to cross a metal step-stile onto the road with a faded Cumbria Coastal Way sign. Go right crossing **Powburgh Beck** (considerable casual car parking scope); looking left from the bridge note the eroded trough banks of the old canal/railway where tracks once were laid. The path slips through a kissing-gate, running inside the pasture with the roadside hedge to a kissing-gate exiting back onto the road, now within the village of **Burgh-by-Sands**.

Exiting the churchyard via the arching yews, note the neighbouring Fort House, affirming the location of Aballava. This house, along with others, reveals the red-and-white-chequered diaper brick-work distinctive of the Carlisle area. The new timber bus shelter is a reminder for walkers that the Hadrian's Wall Bus can be used, either from here or from several places west along the Path. It is a regular means of return to Carlisle.

At the cross-roads note the brown sign directing right along the Sandsfield road to **King Edward I Monument**.

ST MICHAEL'S CHURCH AND ABALLAVA ROMAN FORT

St Michael's showing arrow slits in defended tower

Diagonally opposite, a metal hand-gate gives entry into St Michael's churchyard. A visit to the church is almost obligatory, and certainly essential in the context of the Wall. For best effect go round to the south side and observe the red and grey sandstone blocks of genuine Roman masonry. The church was largely built in the 13th century, perhaps a foot or two higher than the Roman Wall, but what you see is a 'living reincarnation' of the Wall that once ran up to, and from, Aballava Roman fort, situated in this immediate vicinity. There is evidence of three forts in the Burgh area. The fort-name Aballava, referring to 'an apple orchard', may seem unlikely, but it has been calculated that average temperatures in Roman times were five degrees higher than today (even with global warming).

St Michael's is not just a church, it is a social history record from times when there was a greater fear than the fear of God. Following the death of Edward I the entire Anglo-Scottish border erupted into violence, and people sought every means to protect their lives and property. The folk of Burgh sought leave to fortify their church and were in such haste that some parts fell down during the process. Hence, with still abundant Roman Wall-stone in the vicinity, they raised a stoutly buttressed tower with arrow slits, the only access being via an iron gate, called a yatt, from within the nave. Medieval bands of thieving, pillaging and murdering Border reivers met their match here.

The church merits a careful look; inside, on the east wall of the chancel is the carved head of a Roman pagan god. The most beautiful feature of the entire church is the series of stained-glass windows in the north aisle, depicting St Cuthbert with Durham Cathedral, St Aidan with the ruins of Lindisfarne, St Kentigern with St Asaph Cathedral, Edward I with Burgh Church, and St Ninian with the ruins of Whithorn Abbey.

Known as 'The Hammer of the Scots' and instigator of the major stone-built castles in England and Wales, this is a king who reigned down with a passion. He died on Burgh Marshes of dysentery on 7th July 1307 after he had instructed his army to carry his body into action to make yet one more assault on his most hated foe Robert the Bruce; instead the army turned back. It is a little ironic that Robert's father was born at nearby Holm Cultram Abbey. Edward was carried to Burgh church to lie in state before transfer via Lanercost Priory to his last resting place at Westminster Abbey. Probably the ablest soldier-king England ever had, sadly his legacy was a most terrible Border warfare.

Follow the narrow village street, noting Cross Farm's cruck symbol on its name-plate hinting at the clay-dabbin barn which survives still and can be glimpsed through the archway into the backyard. After this, on the right, spot a thatched cruck house; another exists a 100 yards up the

Edward I Monument

The Greyhound

Sandsfield road. Buckbottom Farm is an interesting, if purpose-lost, brick farm courtyard.

Burgh Post Office, selling snacks/ice cream/soft drinks, is located in Fauld Farm opposite **The Greyhound** pub: both of these facilities have proved of great 'comfort value' for Wall walkers! Burgh, pronounced 'bruff ', is a village with a highly developed sense of purpose and vitality; indeed it won the regional 'Village of the Year' award in 2003.

The route continues along the street with its interesting mix of cottages and houses; notice the large sundial on one early 20th-century house. Just before The Stackyard, a new house, its name harking back to the days of corn- and hay-ricks, is a particularly handsome pale green house down a drive to the right with an architecturally intriguing outbuilding. There is little hint of anything remotely Roman, excepting 'Vallum', the house on the right after the footpath to **Watch Hill**.

The tall trees in the vicinity of **Dykesfield House** give rooks plenty of scope for their discordant chatter to ring out. The minor road leading left to Longburgh crosses a metal parapet bridge. Take a look – the lower portion of the stone walling is curved with signs of rope wear on the east side, a legacy of its life as a canal; it was constructed in 1823 (11.25 miles/18km long) and connected Carlisle with coastal trade shipping. The adjacent cottage was built with the canal; there was evidently much heated resentment, for the property was burnt down in 1823 and the culprit never discovered despite the handsome reward of one shilling and six pence! The property has always remained in the same family.

⮕E EASTBOUND 4 The Path crosses the cattle-grid to bid farewell to the salt marshes and follows the road into Burgh-by-Sands. Immediately after the church, watch for the kissing-gate on the left. Follow the roadside hedge down the pasture to exit at a kissing-gate at Powburgh Beck bridge. Keep forward to a metal step-stile on the left. Cross, advancing with a tall hedge on the left to reach a footbridge. Cross and head straight ahead, accompanying the remains of an old lane to a stile, to enter a green lane. This becomes a regular farm track leading into Beaumont; turn right to reach the triangular green.

30/3
Dykesfield ⇄ Drumburgh

*Walking at sea-level, if not
exactly seeing level… The
wonderfully wide backdrop of Scottish
hills deserves a Segedunum-like tower gallery*

Distance: 3 miles/4.8km

◄◄W **WESTBOUND 30** From the Longburgh road junction the scenery undergoes a radical transformation, with the HM Coastguard building behind the new houses a hint of this change. After crossing the cattle-grid the walk embarks upon a three-mile road trod to Drumburgh alongside the great spreading salt-marsh of Burgh Marsh, the summer grazing ground of cattle and sheep. The roadside flood-bank, some five feet up, may look like a good

WARNING: TIDES, FLOODING AND DOGS

Signs stating potential flood depth along the road might look like petty scare-mongering, but they are there because at times the salt marsh is inundated as far as the flood-bank up to the various depths indicated. This tends to occur when spring high tides coincide with heavy rainfall in the hills and a strong westerly wind. Advice on tide levels is readily available: there is a signboard at Dykesfield, tidal information leaflets at local B&Bs and TICs, and information on the Countryside Agency's website: www.nationaltrail.co.uk/hadrianswall. Indeed there is no excuse to be caught out – just remember to allow one hour either side of high tide for your marsh-side march.

At two points, signs direct visitors to the distant foreshore with the necessary warning: danger from fast-flowing tides and quick sands. The tidal Eden comes within view only latterly, so most of the diverse bird-life will be encountered as it flies overhead. The marshes are a Site of Special Scientific Interest, a bird reserve of major importance, so please keep this in mind should you be in a large party or exercising your dog.

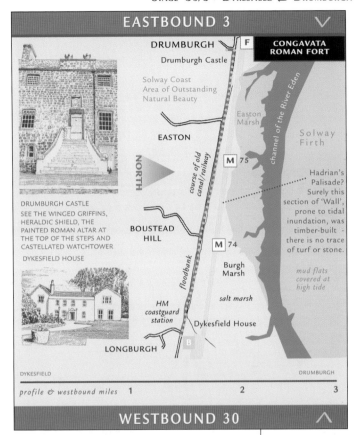

EASTBOUND 3 ⌄

DRUMBURGH

Drumburgh Castle

F | CONGAVATA ROMAN FORT

Solway Coast
Area of Outstanding
Natural Beauty

Easton
Marsh

channel of the River Eden

EASTON

Solway
Firth

M 75

Hadrian's
Palisade?
Surely this
section of 'Wall',
prone to tidal
inundation, was
timber-built -
there is no trace
of turf or stone.

course of old
canal/railway

NORTH ▶

DRUMBURGH CASTLE
SEE THE WINGED GRIFFINS,
HERALDIC SHIELD, THE
PAINTED ROMAN ALTAR AT
THE TOP OF THE STEPS AND
CASTELLATED WATCHTOWER

DYKESFIELD HOUSE

**BOUSTEAD
HILL**

M 74

Burgh
Marsh

*mud flats
covered at
high tide*

floodbank

salt marsh

HM
*coastguard
station*

Dykesfield House

B

LONGBURGH

DYKESFIELD   DRUMBURGH

profile & westbound miles   1   2   3

WESTBOUND 30 ⌃

alternative to the hard tarmac, though birding interests
frown on walkers following the bank-top. Despite being
partially screened by the adjacent hedge, they fear the
important bird-life will be disturbed.

Over the flood-bank ran the canal/railway, now
poorly evidenced. The road rises up short ramps at the
Boustead Hill and Easton road junctions; the former hamlet has its share of distinguished farmhouses and cottages.

*Hadrian's Wall Bus
at Dykesfield*

Boustead means 'farm with a store-house', from its development as a colony of merchants connected with the canal, while Easton means 'eastern farm', being east of Drumburgh.

For all the distance, it is amazing for just how long one hears vehicles crossing the cattle-grid at the

Easton sign

Canal bridge at Dykesfield

Dykesfield end. There is a cattle-grid where Fresh Creek, draining the meadows to the south, slips through to the join the Eden half-way to the Easton junction. At the junction the sign includes the curious name Finglandrigg, which means either 'the finger-shaped long ridge' or 'fair valley ridge' – this latter a plausible combination of Celtic and Norse.

The road crosses the flood-bank and line of the old canal/railway to rise up into the village of **Drumburgh** (pronounced drum'bruff). The name contains Celtic and Old English terms and means 'the flat ridge with fortifications', alluding to the Roman fort of Congavata. Being so close to Maia (Bowness) this was a tiny fort, just two acres; the name is enigmatic.

Pass up by the telephone kiosk and brick farm buildings to comprehend the majestic **Drumburgh Castle**: a

Drumburgh Castle

farmhouse with panache; once again we witness the Wall in a new glorification. In his itinerary of 1539, John Leland referred to it thus: 'Drumburgh ys in ye mudde way betwixt Bolness and Burgh. At Drumburgh the Lord Dacre's father builded upon old ruins a pretty pyle for defence of the country. The stones of the Pict Wall were pulled down to build it.' So there you have it straight from the folklore of the time. In 1307 Edward I granted a royal licence to crenallate the older building, which explains why the farmhouse is called 'Castle'. A fine flight of stone steps leads to the main door; it replaced the original wooden ladder that could easily be withdrawn, thereby making the accommodation awkward for invaders. This is a high-status bastle house – bastles were usually of a far more modest scale. The castelled west end of the roof is a viewing platform commanding a magnificent prospect over the Solway and south to the Lakeland fells.

The wall beneath was in danger of collapse, so in 1978 it was meticulously rebuilt, removing the internal floors and inserting concrete blocking to the inner wall, thus making it secure for another 1000 years at least!

Notice the painted Roman altar and a second one below, artefacts gathered in times past from the site of Congavata. Above the door the decaying stone coats of arms of the Dacre family, griffins with spread wings, are perched; they once included the initials 'TD' for Thomas Dacre. The same family built Naworth Castle.

The hamlet is otherwise less memorable. Walkers will be pleased to know that Grange Farm has set up a self-service stop for their refreshment, most welcome after the long tramp from Burgh. The facility is located on the right after Lowther House, a former pub, up the lane, forking left before Grange farmhouse to the brick farm-shed. Notice the large erratic of Kirkcudbright granite removed from an adjacent field.

↦E EASTBOUND 3 Pass down the road by Drumburgh Castle Farm following the open road beside the salt marsh and crossing two cattle-grids over a distance of three miles to reach Dykesfield. The route is simple and the walking is easy too!

Drumburgh House

31/2
Drumburgh ⇄ Port Carlisle

*Arching back to the
front from a green-pastured Arcadia*

Distance: 3.3 miles/5.3km

◄◄W WESTBOUND 31 The path leaves the centre of Drumburgh, which means 'the defended place on a flat ridge', by the road left passing down by Low Farm. The road becomes a rough pot-holed track through a broad lane. Over to the left is the great expanse of Drumburgh Moss and Whiteholme Common, one of the last remaining raised mires or peat bogs on the Solway Plain, a mosaic of peat, woodland and grassland. This National Nature Reserve accounts for two percent of the total area of this lowland moss habitat in England; it contains 13 species of sphagnum, as well as the carnivorous sundew and a wealth of cotton grass. Lizards and adders find a comfortable haven, as does a wonderful diversity of bird-life from Red grouse and curlew to redshank, Short-eared owl and Grasshopper warblers; huge winter flocks of geese are a speciality.

The rare Large heath butterfly and the impressive day-flying Emperor moth frequent this special place; Hadrian would have approved of the presence of the latter! Evidence of the peat cutting in the parish waste is identified by the bracken growth. A gate intervenes, with **Moss Cottage** visible ahead, but the path bears right into the narrow lane leading by a forlorn combine harvester. The environs of **Walker House Farm** can be muddy when wet; pass on to a small footbridge and kissing-gate. Continue with the stream, right, to a further kissing-gate, and bear half-left to a gated footbridge beside a field-bridge. Keep the hedge to the left, curving with the long narrow pasture to a kissing-gate onto the road in **Glasson**, an Irish name that would appear to mean 'homestead'.

Path at Walker House

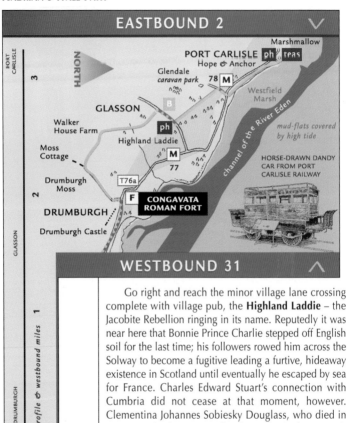

Marshmallow

PORT CARLISLE ph teas
Hope & Anchor

Glendale
caravan park 78 M

Westfield
Marsh

GLASSON

Walker
House Farm

Moss
Cottage

Drumburgh
Moss

DRUMBURGH

Drumburgh Castle

Highland Laddie ph

77 M

T76a

F CONGAVATA
ROMAN FORT

channel of the River Eden

mud-flats covered
by high tide

HORSE-DRAWN DANDY
CAR FROM PORT
CARLISLE RAILWAY

PORT CARLISLE 3 · GLASSON 2 · DRUMBURGH

NORTH

profile & westbound miles 1

Go right and reach the minor village lane crossing complete with village pub, the **Highland Laddie** – the Jacobite Rebellion ringing in its name. Reputedly it was near here that Bonnie Prince Charlie stepped off English soil for the last time; his followers rowed him across the Solway to become a fugitive leading a furtive, hideaway existence in Scotland until eventually he escaped by sea for France. Charles Edward Stuart's connection with Cumbria did not cease at that moment, however. Clementina Johannes Sobiesky Douglass, who died in 1771 at Finsthwaite at the foot of Windermere, is thought to have been his illegitimate daughter, courtesy of his mistress Clementina Walkenshaw. As a place for *en route* refreshment the Highland Laddie serves the walker well. ◄

Go left or, if leaving the pub front door, head straight on! A gated lane leads in harmony with the lost vallum to meet a metalled road at the **Glendale caravan park**. Go right and cross the coast road as did the canal; note the impressive reed-filled section to the right. At a hand-gate

Note: Barrock House, just prior to the pub, which is constructed of red sandstone blocks to Roman Wall specification.

Highland Laddie, Glasson

Canal basin access to breakwater channel

join a sheltered path beside the reconstituted pond, within the old canal-cum-railway bound for Port Carlisle.

For 22 years from 1821 the canal had an important commercial life when Fisher's Cross Quay become the bustling Port Carlisle. Shifting sands and the emergence of the great age of steam spelt an end to its commercial fortunes; the canal was drained and a rail-track installed. At a stroke Port Carlisle was no more.

This railway line was considered to be nothing more than a very minor branch line, subservient to the more lucrative development of Silloth, meaning 'sea-laith' (barn), which catered to the Victorian passion for elegant resorts and bracing sea air. The Scottish, North British Railway Company that ran to Port Carlisle ceased freight in 1899. However, the one horse-drawn coach, 'Dandy no. 1', dating from 1859, survived, and remained in service until the onset of the Great War in 1914. Dandy no. 1 is currently on display at the York Railway Museum. A steam locomotive plied the line for a short period thereafter, but the tracks were lifted and Port Carlisle duly lost

all rail connection, the trackbed becoming either
farmland or a haven for wildlife.

↦E EASTBOUND 2 Upon entry into Port Carlisle the path bears left following the
shore-side track by the Marshmallow tea-room to cross the bridge on the site of
the old canal sea-lock. Passing through successive hand-gates in front of bungalows the path heads on via kissing-gates along a tree-sheltered passage beside the
old canal, passing a glorified hen run to emerge onto the coast road. Cross directly over, following the road to the massive Glendale caravan park; at the entrance
go left along the gated lane in harmony with the course of the vallum. This arrives
in the village of Glasson, with its pub the Highland Laddie. Go right, along the
village street seeking the footpath signed left after the old chapel. Keep the hedge
close right as it curves right to a gated footbridge, and bear half-left to a kissing-
gate. With a stream fence left, advance just one field length to a footbridge
entering a farm lane at Walker House. The hardcore track advances to meet a
lane from Moss Cottage. Bearing left along a broad, pot-holed track, flanked
by scrubby dykes, this duly leads onto a metalled road leading
into Drumburgh.

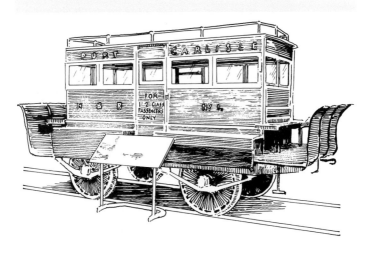

Dandy Car

32/1

Port Carlisle ⇄ *Bowness-on-Solway*

Cheers Hadrian!
Thanks for laying out such a fantastic show!

Distance: 1.1 miles/1.8km

◄◄**W WESTBOUND 32** Passing Solway Chapel proceed via hand-gates; keep to the shore path, passing cottages converted from Dandy horse stables that face directly out upon the breakwater island. Cross a bridge on the site of the canal sea-lock from the basin, from where the wooden steamer pier was formerly extended; a few vestigal wooden stakes remain. This is now a place where bird spotters frequently congregate, telescopes perched upon tripods.

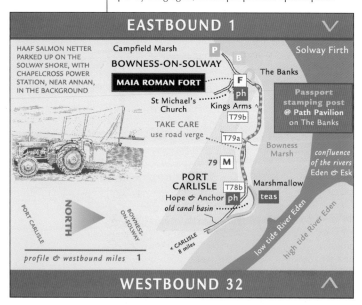

EASTBOUND 1 ∨

HAAF SALMON NETTER PARKED UP ON THE SOLWAY SHORE, WITH CHAPELCROSS POWER STATION, NEAR ANNAN, IN THE BACKGROUND

Campfield Marsh   P   Solway Firth

BOWNESS-ON-SOLWAY   B

MAIA ROMAN FORT   The Banks

F

ph   Passport stamping post @ Path Pavilion on The Banks

St Michael's Church   Kings Arms ∧

T79b

TAKE CARE use road verge   T79a

Bowness Marsh   confluence of the rivers Eden & Esk

79   M

PORT CARLISLE   T78b   Marshmallow

Hope & Anchor ph   teas

old canal basin

PORT CARLISLE   BOWNESS-ON-SOLWAY   **NORTH** ▶   low tide River Eden   high tide River Eden

◄ CARLISLE 8 miles

profile & westbound miles   **1**

WESTBOUND 32 ∧

A track leads by a low stone building, which stands on the site of the original haaf fisherman's dwelling known as Fisher's Cross, the only building in this vicinity prior to the development of the port community. Contemporary with the canal basin, this later building was originally a bath-house to refresh passengers newly disembarked from the high seas.

Haaf Net

The name Fisher's Cross is connected with the living history of the Solway Haaf Net Fishery ('haaf' derives from the old Norse for 'river channel'). For more than 1000 years men have worked their haaf nets, using either the lighter shoal or heavier marsh beam frames, to catch salmon and sea trout. There is a comparable activity on the Annan shore, and on both sides it is a honoured tradition – passed from father to son. Should you call in at the village pub listen out for the contemporary song 'The Green and the Blue' about a fisherman who lost his net in the current, recovering it three days later brim-full of fish!

Next comes the former Customs House. With the arrival of the railway it became the Station House and is now the Marshmallow tea-room, hence its bright confectionery-pink livery.

The track meets the coast road, opposite Hesket House. Above the front door lintel spot a tiny fragment of

Roman altar stone. The inscription is hard to decipher – 'MATRIBUS SUIS MILITE' – and is apparently attributed to a mother goddess. Hesket House was the old Steam Packet Inn where people bound for Whitehaven *en route* to Liverpool and emigration via Ellis Island to the United States lodged while waiting for their passage. ◄

Back along the main street is a fine terrace of 'port' houses. Facing the old navigation basin built by the Earl of Lonsdale in 1819, now with a bowling green in its midst, is Solway House, another boarding house for erstwhile ocean-going travellers. The **Hope & Anchor** is a more than welcome trail-side hostelry.

The Path is now intent on Bowness, that is Bowness-on-Solway not Bowness-on-Windermere – some visitors have been known to be confused by plain 'Bowness'! There is nought but a grass verge for respite, as the route has been obliged to follow the coast road along Bowness Marsh. The broad sweep of the Scottish shore is quite eye-catching. Notice the sequence of pale green sheds; these store munitions, and the earthen banks to the east of each are a precaution lest any one explode and jeopardise its neighbour!

The vestige banking of the Roman Wall is hardly apparent from the road. William Camden, writing in *Britannia*, published in 1586 following his antiquarian foray around the country, commented on the Wall at Bowness: 'I marvailed at first, why they built here so great

The parents of Thomas Woodrow Wilson stayed here: he was a first-generation American citizen when he became the 28th Democratic President, holding office from 1913 to 1921. Woodrow Wilson was a Nobel Peace Prize winner in 1919 and founder of the League of Nations, though the US Senate refused to support it. During his presidency he came to Britain once, when he made an emotional trip to Carlisle to visit the house in which his mother was born.

*Path pavilion at
The Banks*

a fortification, considering that for eight miles or there-abouts, there lieth opposite a very great frith and arme of the sea; but now I understand that very ebbe the water is so low, that the Borderers and beas-stealers [*sic*] may easily wade over.' ▶

Expect no great fanfares on entry into **Bowness-on-Solway**, which means 'the curved promontory'. The road enters the narrow village main street; underneath the tarmac it is beck-stone cobbled. Turn right opposite the Wesleyan Home Mission Chapel. Just before the Post Office, go into an alley leading to **The Banks**, a modest promenade centred upon the Path Pavilion, which is soon to gain a set of informative panels.

The very Roman timber structure sits above a well and garden; this is quite appropriate, for the name derives from the Latin *papilio* meaning 'butterfly tent'. There is access down onto the beach over the sea-wall for that 'ceremonial finish' and the long reflective gaze over the sparkling waters. Perhaps only now the sense of being at the far-flung edge of the Roman Empire strikes home.

The graceful form of Criffel stands to the west, sheltering the mouth of the River Nith near Dumfries.

The channel of the Eden is known as Bowness Wath, meaning 'Bowness ford', though it is a far more serious undertaking to cross this than the Kent estuary in Morecambe Bay.

Open view directly across the Solway from the path pavilion to Burnswark and Chapelcross power station

Snowdrops drift down the banks where the Wall once met up with Maia's north wall

In late winter The Banks are a great drift of snowdrops, and in spring daffodils. The spot where the Wall would have merged with the northern rampart of the Roman fort is now well and truly stolen by the sea.

Northwards there are the four cooling towers of Chapelcross power station (to be closed in 2005), north-east of the old market town of Annan, where Thomas Carlyle, the Victorian man of letters, taught at the Academy. Indeed, the low panorama of pillow hills that has accompanied the path from Burgh Marsh, when lit by a late afternoon sun, looks so inviting – a land of promise, not the foreboding of Roman and reiver ages.

The Solway Firth means 'the ford marked by a pillar fjord'. The pillar in question is thought to be the Lochmaben Stone in the Esk near Gretna, a boulder of Criffel granite which marked the Scottish end of the ford. Geologists find the Solway an interesting feature in itself. Though apparently the estuary of two great rivers, the Esk and the Eden, supplemented by Annanwater and the Nith, its existence owes more to a great coming together of land masses – the same blocks that formed Ireland, though at this point the union was not completed. ◀

The continuing path leads back into the village street close to the invisible site of Maia Roman fort, which covered an area of some seven acres. The fort may have replaced Milecastle 80, of which no trace has been found. The name Maia means 'larger', which might suggest the enlargement of the milecastle.

Turn right and, a matter of yards after a side-street forks left, step through the invisible east gate of the fort; the road complies with the Roman thoroughfare, though only the east and west gates fit perfectly with the modern village road system. The farm buildings on the left resonate with bellowing cattle, quite the mid-town farm, though the intention is to move this livestock operation out of the village.

The **Kings Arms** stands at an internal intersection of the Roman fort; there is a convenient map on the pub wall, but for more precise detail and information a leaflet has been prepared, obtainable in the village. Because the fort was such a distance from a source of good building-stone only the principal buildings and superstructure were stone built. Go down Church Lane, and as the back lane emerges so the road slipped through the fort's south gate.

A few strides more and the truly beautiful church of **St Michael's** comes into view, a pleasurable place to visit

St Michael's Church, Bowness-on-Solway

not only to count the Roman fort stones incorporated into the sturdy building, but to sense the history of place it exudes. The old rectory just beyond is now an appropriately named cosy guest-house. How appropriate to have walked from Wallsend to Wallsend.

Should you stroll westwards out of the village you may visit the Bowness Nature Reserve, GR 206617, one mile west of the village. A leaflet to a one-mile nature trail has been produced by the Cumbria Wildlife Trust. The RSPB have a large interest in **Campfield Marsh**, and have just added the further 200-acre Rogersceugh Farm to their estate on Bowness Common. The botanical diversity of this area of raised lowland peat bog is without question precious, the product of many thousands of years of development; it is a monument to protect every bit as carefully as the 'recent history' of the Roman frontier works.

En route notice a blunt promontory from where a timber-framed railway bridge (at the time the longest in the Britain) once spanned the estuary to Annan, an impressive feat of Victorian construction. The bridge was the crucial link between the Cumberland coal-field and the Lanarkshire ironworks, but its demise came during the particularly cold winter of 1934, when ice floes fatally damaged the central pillars. It was demolished in 1936. Though officially only a railway bridge, it was more than tempting on Sundays, observed as 'dry' in Scotland, for those requiring 'a wee dram' to wander over. As the bridge became unsafe so this pedestrian practice became unsafe, and inevitably someone did come 'off the rails'.

The estuary was also the last resting place of the Bowness church bell. In the days of reiving high-jinx a raiding party from Middlebie sneaked across and removed the bell. However, they were not rewarded, for the inhabitants of Bowness rowed after them with such vigour and in such a rage that it caused the bandits to bail out the bell. The men of Bowness sought reparation, and audaciously stole the Middlebie church bell. So, to this day, each new minister at Middlebie is obliged to write a futile letter requesting the bell's return – shades of the

The setting sun glistening in the Nith estuary of the Solway Firth from The Banks, looking west to Criffel

Elgin Marbles, I fear. However, the story took a new twist only a dozen years ago when Dornock church borrowed the bell for a flower festival and happily returned it to Bowness; it is now a friendship bell.

While many a weary walker's thoughts turn to home, others will doubtless wish to see the whole Roman frontier, beyond the mural section. A further 40 miles of Roman coastal defence system existed as a wooden palisade, and this section can be explored using the Cumbria Coastal Path. Within the Roman context this leads by a series of fortlets and turrets to Maryport (Aluana, meaning 'the shining moon'), where a visit to Senhouse Museum is recommended, and on to the Roman port of Ravenglass, specifically visiting the bathhouse of Walls Castle, which has the tallest extant Roman walls in Britain and was built with exotic imported tile and brickwork.

The Stagecoach Bus Company runs the main local bus network in Cumbria and participates with the Hadrian's Wall Bus service, much to the approbation of Wall walkers. All such transport services are greatly to be applauded, and help to underpin the sustainable philosophy which is beginning to gather momentum amongst those involved along the whole length of the Hadrian's Wall Corridor.

➼**E EASTBOUND 1** Within the Roman Empire Maia Roman fort was the furthest from Rome. As all roads are said to lead to Rome then this first leg to Port Carlisle has some significance. Indeed, to start from here one may be expected to walk on to Arbeia (South Shields) and catch an imaginary boat bound for the Mediterranean. The first duty of the Wall-wide walker is to visit the path Pavilion on The Banks. The alley approach is prominently signposted off the main street. Leave by the eastern side-path, and rejoin the street, going left through the narrows to come alongside the railed foreshore road. There is no option at present but the grassy verges beside Bowness Marsh. This is an early opportunity to study the running waters, in which there are occasional sightings of basking shark and porpoise. However, you are more likely to see the marvellous diversity of birds that use this as a conduit through-route along the line of Hadrian's Wall to the Northumberland coast and the North Sea. Spot waders including oystercatchers, redshank and curlew, along with geese (barnacle and greylag) and ducks, such as shelduck and the predatory gull the skua. The range of bird-life, migratory and vagrant, is quite unpredictably exciting. The mile to Port Carlisle a happy mix of stops and starts...so it's light lunch at the Marshmallow or Hope & Anchor, then?

APPENDIX 1
Bibliography

BOOKS (* choose at least one of these to take with you on your walk)

Alcock, Joan, *Life in Roman Britain*, English Heritage/Batsford, 1996

* Bedoyere, Guy de la, *Hadrian's Wall: History and Guide*, Tempus, 1998

Bidwell, Paul, *Hadrian's Wall 1989–99*, South Shields, 1999

* Breeze, David J. and Dobson, Brian, *Hadrian's Wall*, 5th ed, Penguin, 2004

Crow, James, *Books of Housesteads*, English Heritage/Batsford, 1995

Crow, James and Woodside, Robert, *Hadrian's Wall, An Historical Landscape*, National Trust, 1999

Davies, Hunter, *A Walk along the Wall*, Weidenfeld and Nicolson, 1984

Embleton, Ronald, *Hadrian's Wall in the Days of the Romans*, Frank Graham, 1984

Hutton, William, *The First Man to Walk Hadrian's Wall, 1802*, Frank Graham, 1990

* Johnson, Stephen, *Hadrian's Wall*, Batsford/English Heritage, 1989

McCarthy, Mike, *Roman Carlisle and the Lands of the Solway*, Tempus, 2002

Wilmott, Tony, *Birdoswald Roman Fort: 1800 years on Hadrian's Wall*, Tempus, 2001

The Essential Guide to Hadrian's Wall Path, Hadrian's Wall Path Trust, annually updated

MAPS

Harvey Maps, HADRIAN'S WALL PATH
National Trail Map, detailed waterproof map – perfect for all walkers

Ordnance Survey, HADRIAN'S WALL, Historical Map & Guide
Suitable for casual visitors and keen monument-hunters alike

Ordnance Survey, MAP OF HADRIAN'S WALL, 1972 edition.
Only found (all too rarely, as they are treasured) in second-hand book-shops; this is the best map for walkers with a serious landscape history and Wall-intent.

Landranger (1:50,000): 85, 86, 87, 88
Explorer (1:25,000): 314, 315, 316

OTHER READING
Raymond Huneysett, *Archaeologia Aeliana* (1980), vol. VIII
      (study of the legions' construction of the Wall)
News from Hadrian's Wall World Heritage Site – a free magazine
      published by English Heritage three times/year April/August/
      December

APPENDIX 2
Further Information

The guide produced by the Hadrian's Wall Tourism Partnership
(for accommodation)

The Essential Guide to Hadrian's Wall, published by the Hadrian's Wall Path Trust
(for practical advice)

Hadrian's Wall Information Line, tel: 01434 322002;
email haltwhistle@btconnect.com.

APPENDIX 3
Route Summary

	Chapter	Miles	Kilometres
1	Wallsend ⇄ Walker Riverside Park	2.3	3.7
2	Walker Riverside Park ⇄ Elswick	2.9	4.6
3	Elswick ⇄ Denton Dene	2.5	4.0
4	Denton Dene ⇄ Newburn	1.8	2.9
5	Newburn ⇄ Heddon-on-the-Wall	3.8	6.0
6	Heddon-on-the-Wall ⇄ Harlow Hill	4.0	6.4
7	Harlow Hill ⇄ Woodhouses Road-End	2.25	3.5
8	Woodhouses Road-End ⇄ Halton Shields	1.9	3.3
9	Halton Shields ⇄ the Portgate	1.4	2.2
10	The Portgate ⇄ Heavenfield	3.1	5.0
11	Heavenfield ⇄ Chollerford	3.8	6.0
12	Chollerford ⇄ Tower Tye	2.1	3.4
13	Tower Tye ⇄ Carrawburgh	2.1	3.4
14	Carrawburgh ⇄ Sewingshields Farm	2.1	3.4
15	Sewingshields Farm ⇄ Housesteads	2.0	3.2
16	Housesteads ⇄ Steel Rigg	3.1	5.0
17	Steel Rigg ⇄ Cawfields Quarry	3.0	5.0
18	Cawfields Quarry ⇄ Walltown Crags	3.2	5.1
19	Walltown Quarry ⇄ Gilsland	3.9	6.3
20	Gilsland ⇄ Birdoswald	1.3	2.0
21	Birdoswald ⇄ Banks	2.3	3.7
22	Banks ⇄ Walton	3.7	6.0
23	Walton ⇄ Newtown	2.0	3.2
24	Newtown ⇄ Oldwall	1.8	2.9
25	Oldwall ⇄ Crosby-on-Eden	3.2	5.1
26	Crosby-on-Eden ⇄ Eden Bridge	4.3	6.9
27	Eden Bridge ⇄ Grinsdale	3.1	5.0
28	Grinsdale ⇄ Beaumont	1.9	3.0
29	Beaumont ⇄ Dykesfield	2.4	3.9
30	Bykesfield ⇄ Brumburgh	3.0	4.8
31	Drumburgh ⇄ Port Carlisle	3.3	5.3
32	Port Carlisle ⇄ Bowness-on-Solway	1.1	1.8
	Total:	**84.65**	**136**

APPENDIX 4
Contact Details

There is an extremely strong tourism partnership working within the Hadrian's Wall corridor. All the organisations detailed below, as well as Northumberland National Park, English Heritage, the National Trust, Solway AONB, the Countryside Agency, local businesses, city councils (Newcastle and Carlisle councils and the district councils along the course of the route), Cumbria Tourist Board and One Northeast (now incorporating Northumbria Tourist Board) are involved and have relevant information available.

Hadrian's Wall Information Line
Tel. 01434 322002
Email haltwhistle@btconnect.com
This facility has been established to act as a conduit for visitors (especially walkers). It is the main contact for up-to-date information, particularly accommodation.

Websites
Hadrian's Wall Tourism Partnership, www.hadrians-wall.org

Countryside Agency, www.national-trail.co.uk/hadrianswall

Museums
Senhouse
(Maryport) tel. 01900 816168, www.senhousemuseum.co.uk

Tullie House (Carlisle)
tel. 01228 534781, www.tulliehouse.co.uk

Birdoswald Roman Fort (Gilsland)
tel. 016977 47602, www.birdoswaldromanfort.org

Carvoran Roman Army Museum (Greenhead) (Owned by the Vindolanda Trust), tel. 016977 47485,

www.vindolanda.com
Vindolanda Fort and Museum, tel. 01434 344277, www.vindolanda.com

Housesteads Roman Fort, tel. 01434 344363, www.english-heritage.org.uk

Chesters Roman Fort, tel. 01434 681379, www.english-heritage.org.uk

Corbridge Roman Site, tel. 01434 632349, www.english-heritage.org.uk

Museum of Antiquities (Newcastle), entry free, tel. 0191 222 7846/7849, www.museums.ncl.ac.uk

Segedunum Roman Fort and Museum (Wallsend) tel. 0191 2369347, www.twmuseums.org.uk

Arbeia Roman Fort and Museum (South Shields) tel. 0191 4561369, www.twmuseums.org.uk

Tourist Information Centres
Whitehaven TIC, Market Hill, Whitehaven CA28 7JG, tel. 01946 852939

Carlisle TIC, Visitor Centre,
Greenmarket, Carlisle CA3 8JH,
tel. 01228 625600

Haltwhistle TIC, The Railway Station,
Station Road, Haltwhistle NE49 0AH,
tel. 01434 322002

Hexham TIC, Wentworth Car Park,
Hexham NE46 1XE,
tel. 01434 652220

Newcastle TIC, 128 Grainger Street,
Newcastle-upon-Tyne NE1 5AF, tel.
0191 2778000

Youth Hostels and Camping Barns (campingbarns@yha.org.uk)
Carlisle, tel. 0870 770 5752
Bankshead Camping Barn,
tel. 0870 770 6113

Greenhead, tel. 0870 770 5842

Once Brewed, tel. 0870 770 5980

Acomb, tel. 0870 770 5664

Newcastle-upon-Tyne,
tel. 0870 770 5972

Public Transport
Traveline, tel. 0870 608 2608

National Rail Enquiries,
tel. 08457 48 49 50

Journey Planner,
www.jplanner.org.uk

National Rail,
www. nationalrail.co.uk

GNER (London-Newcastle),
www.gner.co.uk

Arriva Trains
(Newcastle, Manchester, Settle-
Carlisle),
www.rrne.co.uk
Virgin Trains,
www.virgintrains.co.uk

APPENDIX 5

Hadrian's Wall Bus AD122

Carlisle · Brampton · Haltwhistle · Hexham

The principal pick-up/drop-off points from east to west:

WALLSEND, METRO INTERCHANGE, NEAR SEGEDUNUM
NEWCASTLE, CENTRAL STATION
HEDDON-ON-THE-WALL, TOWNE GATE
CORBRIDGE, HILL STREET
CORBRIDGE, ROMAN SITE – (CORSTOPITUM)
HEXHAM, TOURIST INFORMATION CENTRE
HEXHAM, RAILWAY STATION
CHESTERS ROMAN FORT
HOUSESTEADS ROMAN FORT
ONCE BREWED NATIONAL PARK CENTRE
VINDOLANDA ROMAN FORT
TWICE BREWED INN
MILECASTLE INN
HALTWHISTLE, RAILWAY STATION
CARVORAN ROMAN ARMY MUSEUM
GREENHEAD
GILSLAND
BIRDOSWALD ROMAN FORT
LANERCOST PRIORY
BRAMPTON, MARKET PLACE
CROSBY-ON-EDEN
CARLISLE, ENGLISH STREET
CARLISLE, TULLIE HOUSE
BOWNESS-ON-SOLWAY

THE BUS ALSO PICKS UP/DROPS OFF AT THE FOLLOWING POINTS:

BETWEEN WALLSEND AND HEXHAM

Byker – Shields Road/Potts Road, Newcastle General Hospital (West Road), Plaza Bingo Hall, Fox and Hounds Inn, Denton Burn, Lemington Road End, Bulcher Social Club, Walbottle Campus, Throckley roundabout, Royal French Arms, Heddon Three Tuns, Harlow Hill, Robin Hood, Errington Arms.

BETWEEN HEXHAM AND CARLISLE

Acomb, Brunton crossroads, Chollerford roundabout, Longbyre, Crosby-on-Eden.

BETWEEN CARLISLE AND BOWNESS-ON-SOLWAY

Kirkandrews-on-Eden, Beaumont, Burgh-by-Sands, Boustead Hill, Drumburgh, Glasson, Port Carlisle.

The timetable is subject to change
The bus has scope to carry a bike
'Hail and Ride' has been abolished

A GUIDE TO YOUR RIDE

The Wall bus runs between Hexham and Carlisle, the 'great border city'. Carlisle lies at the pivotal part of two features marking the border between England and Scotland: to the north of the city is the Solway Firth, overwhich lies Scotland, whilst to the east runs the famous Roman military march of Hadrian's Wall. The features of the route of the Hadrian's Wall Bus between Carlisle and Hexham are described here, helping you to relish the great monument in the richness of its landscape setting. Visitors are rightly aware of the historic importance of the Roman Wall, after all it is a World Heritage Site and the bus which travells from Walsend to Bowness on Solway allows easy to access to many of its most significant parts.

This unique pictorial guide covers the middle section of the Hadrian's Wall bus route, which operates on a regular basis during the summer months. It is split into three scenic stages, orientated eastward from Carlisle to Hexham, a distance of 70km/44 miles (intermediate bus stops in bold). The pictures appear in sequence, and to help you anticipate where to look, each has a box giving the location and view directions: L (left), R (right), A (ahead) and B (backwards).

SCENIC STAGE 1: Carlisle to Brampton – 18km/11 miles

The bus makes a stirring start, circulating through the main streets of the city passing down Lowther Street to enter Castleway. Briefly halting at the superb **Tullie House Museum and Art Gallery**, with its Millennium Gallery and Rotunda vantage to the Castle. The bus heads west, beyond the Irish Gate gantry bridge, crossing the River Caldew, to switch back at the roundabout beside McVities, home for 170 years of biscuit-makers Carrs of Carlisle. Re-viewing the battlements of Carlisle Castle the bus crosses the River Eden to enter Stanwix bearing right into Brampton Road.

Hidden beneath the churchyard and houses to the left is the site of Petriana, the largest cavalry fort outside of Rome, with stabling for a thousand horsemen and headquarters of the senior commanding officer for the Wall. Glimpsing the Eden meadows of Rickerby Park to the right, a suburban passage is soon replaced by broad country vistas after crossing the M6 motorway. The bus diverts into the charming little village of **Crosby-on-Eden** aligned to the Stanegate. Just short of Crosby Lodge, as the bus advances to rejoin the main road, a sunken section of the pre-Hadrian military way may be spotted to the right; this Roman road spanned the neck of Britannia from Carlisle to Corbridge. Heading east by Carlisle Airport, by the Golden Fleece Inn we cross the River Irthing for the first of three occasions. Its peaty waters influenced by the great conifer forest of Spadeadam at its source.

The Eden plain affords generous views half-left to the Bewcastle Fells, half-right to the sandy knolls about the River Gelt backed by the northernmost summits of the Pennine range culminating upon Cold Fell. Approaching Brampton we leave cultivated farmland and enter a landscape of permanent pasture. As the bus turns into the town towards the red sandstone parish church of St Martin's, far-famed for its superb Pre-Raphaelite stained glass windows, notice the white statue of Hadrian Augustus Aelius, the surest sign yet that we are entering Roman Wall Country.

THE EASTERN WING OF THE IMPRESSIVE TWIN-BARRELLED CITADEL BUILT IN 1810, REPLICATES A FORMER FORTRESS BUILT ON THIS SITE IN 1541.

ARCH REPLICATES LOWTHER CASTLE, NEAR PENRITH, FORMER SEAT OF THE EARLS OF LONSDALE. THE 7TH EARL, LORD LIEUTENANT OF CUMBERLAND AND WESTMORLAND 1802-44

English Street **R**

BUILT TO GUARD THE WEST END OF THE SCOTTISH BORDER, IT WAS ORIGINALLY ERECTED IN TIMBER BY RUFUS IN 1092. THE SCOTS TOOK CONTROL FROM 1135, BUT IN 1157 IT REVERTED TO THE ENGLISH CROWN UNDER HENRY II WHEN THE KEEP AND CURTAIN WALL OF THE CASTLE WERE BUILT MAINLY WITH STONE FROM HADRIAN'S WALL. THAT THEY HAVE SURVIVED TO TODAY INDICATES THEIR STRENGTH.

CURTAIN WALL

KEEP

Castleway **L**

THESE STEPS LEAD DOWN TO THE TULLIE HOUSE MILLENNIUM GALLERY, SET INTO THE CASTLE DITCHES BENEATH THE DUAL CARRIAGEWAY

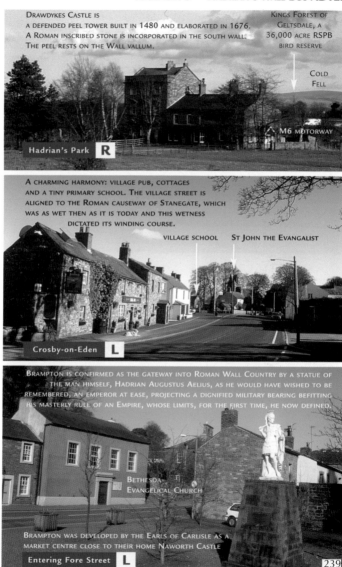

DRAWDYKES CASTLE IS
A DEFENDED PEEL TOWER BUILT IN 1480 AND ELABORATED IN 1676.
A ROMAN INSCRIBED STONE IS INCORPORATED IN THE SOUTH WALL.
THE PEEL RESTS ON THE WALL VALLUM.

KINGS FOREST OF
GELTSDALE, A
36,000 ACRE RSPB
BIRD RESERVE

COLD
FELL

M6 MOTORWAY

Hadrian's Park R

A CHARMING HARMONY: VILLAGE PUB, COTTAGES
AND A TINY PRIMARY SCHOOL. THE VILLAGE STREET IS
ALIGNED TO THE ROMAN CAUSEWAY OF STANEGATE, WHICH
WAS AS WET THEN AS IT IS TODAY AND THIS WETNESS
DICTATED ITS WINDING COURSE.

VILLAGE SCHOOL   ST JOHN THE EVANGALIST

Crosby-on-Eden L

BRAMPTON IS CONFIRMED AS THE GATEWAY INTO ROMAN WALL COUNTRY BY A STATUE OF
THE MAN HIMSELF, HADRIAN AUGUSTUS AELIUS, AS HE WOULD HAVE WISHED TO BE
REMEMBERED, AN EMPEROR AT EASE, PROJECTING A DIGNIFIED MILITARY BEARING BEFITTING
HIS MASTERLY RULE OF AN EMPIRE, WHOSE LIMITS, FOR THE FIRST TIME, HE NOW DEFINED.

BETHESDA
EVANGELICAL CHURCH

BRAMPTON WAS DEVELOPED BY THE EARLS OF CARLISLE AS A
MARKET CENTRE CLOSE TO THEIR HOME NAWORTH CASTLE

Entering Fore Street L

239

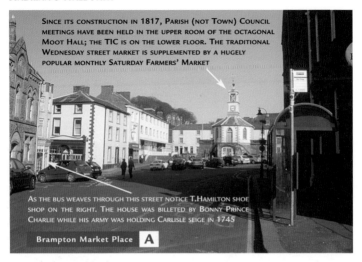

SINCE ITS CONSTRUCTION IN 1817, PARISH (NOT TOWN) COUNCIL MEETINGS HAVE BEEN HELD IN THE UPPER ROOM OF THE OCTAGONAL MOOT HALL; THE TIC IS ON THE LOWER FLOOR. THE TRADITIONAL WEDNESDAY STREET MARKET IS SUPPLEMENTED BY A HUGELY POPULAR MONTHLY SATURDAY FARMERS' MARKET

AS THE BUS WEAVES THROUGH THIS STREET NOTICE T.HAMILTON SHOE SHOP ON THE RIGHT. THE HOUSE WAS BILLETED BY BONNY PRINCE CHARLIE WHILE HIS ARMY WAS HOLDING CARLISLE SEIGE IN 1745

Brampton Market Place **A**

SCENIC STAGE 2:

Brampton to Haltwhistle – 20km/13 miles

With attention fixed on the handsome Moot Hall, the bus leaves the Market Square heading for the peaceful vale of the River Irthing, passing under the wooded Moat and Brampton Rigg. The road dips by the twin-arched Abbey Bridge to halt at the entrance to **Lanercost Priory**. Winding up to the village of Banks, the earthworks of the Wall are encountered and soon the first tumultous viewpoint is met at **Banks Turret**. This commands a wonderful southward prospect towards the Pennine fells. The ridge-top road is followed for much of its course along the original line of the wall. A consistent stretch of Wall heralds the arrival at **Birdoswald Roman Fort**. The bus winds down to **Gilsland** and enters Northumberland, crossing the Tyne watershed near **Longbyre**. The bus then enters Northumberland National Park on leaving **Greenhead** on the climb with the B6318 to Carvoran and **Walltown Quarry**. Then, turning back onto the Military Road, we divert down into the South Tyne valley to reach Haltwhistle, the mid-point of our journey and demonstrably the centre of Britain!

COURSE OF HADRIAN'S WALL ALONG HORIZON

THE ELEGANT TWIN-ARCHED **ABBEY BRIDGE** (PEDESTRIAN ONLY) THE PROSAIC REPLACEMENT TO THE RIGHT IS USED ON OUR SECOND CROSSING OF THE IRTHING

ROAD TO NAWORTH CASTLE, SEAT OF THE HOWARD FAMILY (EARLS OF CARLISLE) SINCE 1604. THE HOWARD'S PRINCIPAL HOME IS CASTLE HOWARD IN YORKSHIRE

Abbey Bridge **A**

ABBEY MILL LAST MILLED OATS IN THE 1920S, BUILT C.1783 BY THE EARL OF CARLISLE, HARNESSING QUARRY BECK

Lanercost **R**

KING EDWARD I LODGED IN THE TOWER WING OF THE VICARAGE DURING THE FINAL SIX MONTHS OF HIS LIFE IN 1306, WHEN THE ENGLISH COURT WAS HELD AT LANERCOST PRIORY. RED AND GREY SANDSTONE WALL STONE DOMINATE THE CONSTRUCTION OF THE PRIORY, ADJACENT VICARAGE, THE FOREGROUND GATE ARCH AND THE BOUNDING WALL (LEFT OF THIS PICTURE).

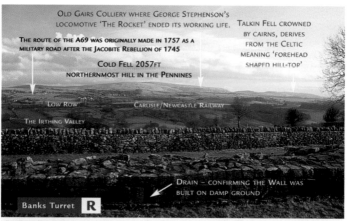

OLD GAIRS COLLIERY WHERE GEORGE STEPHENSON'S LOCOMOTIVE 'THE ROCKET' ENDED ITS WORKING LIFE.

TALKIN FELL CROWNED BY CAIRNS, DERIVES FROM THE CELTIC MEANING 'FOREHEAD SHAPED HILL-TOP'

THE ROUTE OF THE A69 WAS ORIGINALLY MADE IN 1757 AS A MILITARY ROAD AFTER THE JACOBITE REBELLION OF 1745

COLD FELL 2057FT NORTHERNMOST HILL IN THE PENNINES

LOW ROW

CARLISLE/NEWCASTLE RAILWAY

THE IRTHING VALLEY

DRAIN – CONFIRMING THE WALL WAS BUILT ON DAMP GROUND

Banks Turret **R**

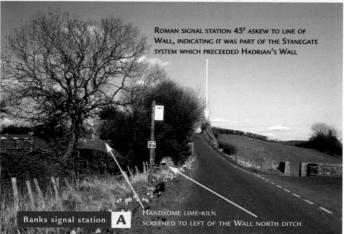

ROMAN SIGNAL STATION 45° ASKEW TO LINE OF WALL, INDICATING IT WAS PART OF THE STANEGATE SYSTEM WHICH PRECEEDED HADRIAN'S WALL

Banks signal station **A**

HANDSOME LIME-KILN SCREENED TO LEFT OF THE WALL NORTH DITCH

HERE SEE ONE OF THE SEQUENCE OF SPECIAL HADRIAN'S WALL BUS STOPS ENCOUNTERED ON THE SERVICE FROM CARLISLE TO HEXHAM. ONLY AT THESE POINTS CAN YOU JOIN OR LEAVE THE BUS – BUT FOR REASONS OF SAFETY PASSENGERS NO LONGER CAN HAIL & RIDE. THE WALL-WIDE SERVICE WHICH RUNS ONLY ONCE A DAY AT PRESENT FROM SEGEDUNUM TO BOWNESS-ON-SOLWAY USES THE REGULAR BUS STOPS OF LOCAL, NORMALLY YEAR-ROUND, SERVICES.

LEAHILL FARM, WITH LOCALLY CHARACTERISTIC RED-PAINTED COW-BYRE DOORS

LINE OF ROMAN WALL

LEAHILL TURRET 51B, LOOK OUT FOR PIPER SIKE TURRET 51A, AFTER A FURTHER THIRD-OF-A-MILE

LINE OF WALL SUPPLY CHARIOTWAY

Leahill **B**

THE VIEW BELOW ILLUSTRATES THE DIFFERENT STAGES OF THE CONSTRUCTION OF THE WALL

FROM THE RIVER IRTHING, IMMEDIATELY EAST OF BIRDOSWALD, TO BOWNESS-ON-SOLWAY THE ORIGINAL ROMAN WALL WAS CONSTRUCTED AS A TURF BANK, POSSIBLY WITH TIMBER PALISADING. SOME TIME LATER THE CONSTRUCTION OF A STRONGER MILITARY LINE WAS DEMANDED AND SANDSTONE WAS HAULED ON SLEDS INTO THE WETTER WESTERN SECTOR FOR THE STONE-BUILT WALL. WE CAN SEE THE POINT OF UNION 100 YARDS EAST OF WALL BOWERS.

LINE OF STONE WALL

LINE OF TURF WALL

NORTH DITCH OF THE STONE-BUILT WALL

NORTH DITCH OF THE TURF-BUILT WALL

Wall Bowers **A**　THE POINT WHERE THE TURF AND STONE WALL MERGED

GILLALEES BEACON
(ROMAN SIGNAL STATION)
A FIRE WAS LIT, AMERICAN INDIAN FASHION,
TO WARN OF ADVANCING CALEDONIAN MARAUDERS

SPADEADAM FOREST

LINE OF THE MAIDEN WAY, THE ROMAN ROAD TO BEWCASTLE,
AN OUTPOST SCOUT FORT MARSHALLING THE VULNERABLE WESTERN APPROACHES.

Birdoswald **L**

NINE NICKS OF THIRLWALL (THREE GAPS HAVE BEEN LOST TO QUARRYING)

MUCKLEBANK CRAG
'THE BIG SLOPE'

WALLTOWN QUARRY COUNTRY PARK

SET INTO THE WALL ARE SCULPTED
ROMAN 'GOOD LUCK'
AND CENTURION STONES,
AND AN ELABORATE DRAIN

HADRIAN'S WALL PATH NATIONAL TRAIL
TO WILLOWFORD MILLENNIUM FOOTBRIDGE
CROSSING THE RIVER IRTHING

Birdoswald **A**

WILLOWFORD FARM

NATIONAL TRAIL
MILLENNIUM FOOTBRIDGE

BIRDOSWALD
ROMAN FORT

ROMAN BRIDGE ABUTMENTS

RIVER IRTHING, WHICH MEANS
'THE EARTH-COLOURED RIVER'
ENRICHED BY THE MIRE PEAT
FROM SPADEADAM FOREST.

The Hill **R**

Hadrians Wall
Poltross Burn
Milecastle

THE POLTROSS BURN MILECASTLE
MIRACULOUSLY SURVIVED THE ARRIVAL OF THE
RAILWAY – HISTORIC MONUMENTS WERE NOT
CONSIDERED WORTHY OF PROTECTION AT
THAT TIME!

IN VIEW FROM THE BUS STOP, SITUATED ABOVE
THE POPPING STONE IN THE IRTHING GORGE,
IS GILSLAND SPA HOTEL WHERE SIR WALTER
SCOTT REPUTEDLY POPPED THE QUESTION
TO HIS FUTURE WIFE, CHARLOTTE

Gilsland **L**

OF HADRIAN'S WALL, ONLY THE NORTH
DITCH REMAINS AS THE FINE MASONRY
WAS 'BORROWED' FOR THE CONSTRUCTION
OF THIRLWALL CASTLE

FORMER COLLIERY TERRACE

Willowford Crag

CARVORAN ROMAN ARMY MUSEUM
AND SITE OF THE ONLY JOINT
STANEGATE AND ROMAN WALL FORT

vallum

THE IMPRESSIVE CURTAIN WALLS OF THIRLWALL
CASTLE, WHICH MEANS 'HOLE OR GAP IN THE WALL'
STANDING ABOVE THE TIPALT BURN, HAS
RECENTLY RECEIVED RESTORATIVE WORKS AND MERITS A VISIT.

Longbyre **A**

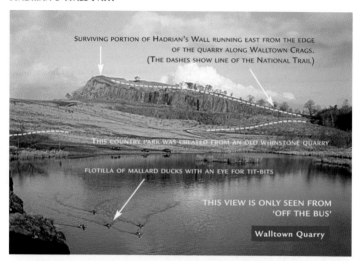

SURVIVING PORTION OF HADRIAN'S WALL RUNNING EAST FROM THE EDGE OF THE QUARRY ALONG WALLTOWN CRAGS. (THE DASHES SHOW LINE OF THE NATIONAL TRAIL)

THIS COUNTRY PARK WAS CREATED FROM AN OLD WHINSTONE QUARRY

FLOTILLA OF MALLARD DUCKS WITH AN EYE FOR TIT-BITS

THIS VIEW IS ONLY SEEN FROM 'OFF THE BUS'

Walltown Quarry

HAVING KEPT CLOSE COMPANY WITH THE ROMAN WALL SINCE BANKS THE BUS TURNS OFF THE MILITARY ROAD TO REACH HALTWHISTLE, AN IMPORTANT CENTRE OF THE WALL COUNTRY

THE TOWN-NAME HALTWHISTLE HAS NOTHING TO DO WITH A WHISTLE-STOP IMPERATIVE TO HALT THE NEWCASTLE TO CARLISLE TRAIN (THOUGH IT DOES STOP!), IT MEANS 'THE MEETING OF STREAMS BENEATH A HILL'. THE TOWN'S TOURIST INFORMATION CENTRE IS SITUATED IN THE OLD TICKET OFFICE.

Haltwhistle Station L

SCENIC STAGE 3: Haltwhistle to Hexham – 32km/20 miles

Climbing back out of the South Tyne valley we rejoin the Military Road at the **Milecastle Inn**. Heading east glimpse the Wall riding the Whin Sill ridge crossing Winshields Crag, the highest point on the frontier at 345 metres. The bus halts at the **Twice Brewed Inn** and turning at **Once Brewed National Park Information Centre** embarks upon a spur to **Vindolanda**, approaching and backtracking along a characteristically straight stretch of Roman road, which is actually older than Hadrian's Wall (though the tarmac is only as old as the bus!). Once again eastbound along the Military Road, we call by **Housesteads** and as the Whin Sill recedes, the road, which consumed the Wall as hardcore, runs tight by the vallum and north ditches via Brocolitia and Limestone Corner before descending to **Chesters** and the Chollerford crossing of the North Tyne. Turning south we catch a glimpse of the Brunton Turret before passing through the villages of Wall and Acomb to enter the handsome town of **Hexham**, regally set upon a knoll overlooking the Tyne.

PEEL TOWER, TO WHICH A THREE-STOREY EXTENSION WAS ADDED IN 19TH CENTURY. THERE IS A CLUSTER OF FIVE BASTLE HOUSES CLOSE TO THE HOTEL, EACH IDENTIFIED BY THESE BLUE WALL-PLAQUES

Haltwhistle **L**

THE COLOURFUL HISTORY OF THE AREA IS GRAPHICALLY PORTRAYED IN THIS FAMOUS HOTEL SIGN WHICH IS REPLICATED AT THE ENTRY TO THE TOWN

THE PUB IS NAMED AFTER MILECASTLE 42A, ABOVE CAWFIELDS QUARRY, PRECARIOUSLY SET ON TILTED GROUND, IT CONTROLLED CALEDONIAN TRAFFIC THROUGH THE ROMAN HOLE GAP GATE-WAY – DEFINITELY A SECTION OF WALL TO VISIT FROM THIS BUS STOP (VIEWED OFF TO THE RIGHT).

STANEGATE ROMAN MARCHING CAMP ABOVE HALTWHISTLE BURN, ONE OF AN UNUSUALLY INTENSIVE CLUSTER OF FORTS IN THIS AREA SUGGESTING AN IMPORTANT CROSS-ROADS, POSSIBLY INFLUENCED BY THE EASILY ACCESSED DEPOSITS OF COAL.

GREAT CHESTERS FARM ON THE SITE OF AESICA ROMAN FORT

MILITARY ROAD MADE IN 1757

Milecastle Inn **A**

CAUSEWAY HOUSE, LANDMARK TRUST PROPERTY WITH HEATHER-THATCHED ROOF

18TH-CENTURY COLLIERS MEMORIAL PILLAR

BARCOMBE HILL WITH ROMAN SIGNAL STATION AND QUARRY

STUMP REMAINS OF IN-SITU ROMAN MILESTONE BESIDE THE TYPICALLY DIRECT ROMAN METALLED CAUSEWAY, LATER DUBBED THE STANEGATE, SEEN HERE LEADING TO VINDOLANDA.

VISIT VINDOLANDA AND SEE FOR YOURSELVES THE 'WRITING TABLETS' WHICH WERE VOTED THE TOP HIS-TORIC TREASURE IN BRITAIN BY THE BRITISH MUSEUM. WITH MORE THAN 1900 DECIPHERED, THEY REVEAL THE DAILY AFFAIRS OF ROMAN LIFE – AND ARE PRICELESS!

Road to Vindolanda **A**

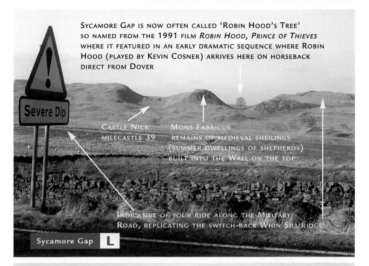

SYCAMORE GAP IS NOW OFTEN CALLED 'ROBIN HOOD'S TREE' SO NAMED FROM THE 1991 FILM *ROBIN HOOD, PRINCE OF THIEVES* WHERE IT FEATURED IN AN EARLY DRAMATIC SEQUENCE WHERE ROBIN HOOD (PLAYED BY KEVIN COSNER) ARRIVES HERE ON HORSEBACK DIRECT FROM DOVER

Severe Dip

CASTLE NICK MILECASTLE 39

MONS FABRICUS REMAINS OF MEDIEVAL SHEILINGS (SUMMER DWELLINGS OF SHEPHERDS) BUILT INTO THE WALL ON THE TOP

INDICATIVE OF YOUR RIDE ALONG THE MILITARY ROAD, REPLICATING THE SWITCH-BACK WHIN SILL RIDGE

Sycamore Gap **L**

EARLY 19TH-CENTURY LIMEKILN WITH GOTHIC ARCH BACKED BY A BAND OF LIMESTONE. COAL, LOCALLY PLENTIFUL, WAS BURNT WITH THE LIMESTONE TO CREATE, WHEN MIXED WITH WATER, SLACKED LIME. THIS WAS APPLIED TO THE FIELDS TO REDUCE ACIDITY, IMPROVING STOCK GRAZING AND GREATLY INCREASING HERBAGE FOR THE HAY CROP.

RAPISHAW GAP   LIMEKILN

CUDDY'S CRAG

LINE OF VALLUM

Carlisle 25 B 6318   Newcastle 32 B 6318

Greenhead 7   Housesteads 1 Chollerford 9

Bardon Mill turn **L**

THE ROMAN WALL RUNS ALONG THE NEAR SKYLINE. CUDDY'S CRAG DERIVES FROM THE PET-NAME OF CUTHBERT. ST CUTHBERT OF HOLY ISLAND: HIS MONKS CREATED THE BEAUTIFULLY ILLUMINATED LINDISFARNE GOSPELS, AND HIS PROTECTION OF EIDER DUCKS AND GREY SEALS MAKE HIM ONE OF THE EARLIEST NATURE CONSERVATIONISTS.

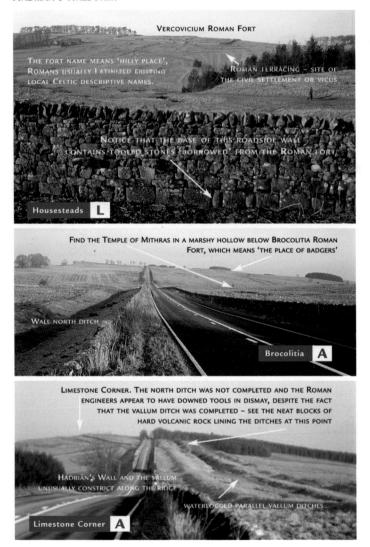

VERCOVICIUM ROMAN FORT

THE FORT NAME MEANS 'HILLY PLACE',
ROMANS USUALLY LATINIZED EXISTING
LOCAL CELTIC DESCRIPTIVE NAMES.

ROMAN TERRACING – SITE OF
THE CIVIL SETTLEMENT OR VICUS

NOTICE THAT THE BASE OF THIS ROADSIDE WALL
CONTAINS TOOLED STONES 'BORROWED' FROM THE ROMAN FORT

Housesteads **L**

FIND THE TEMPLE OF MITHRAS IN A MARSHY HOLLOW BELOW BROCOLITIA ROMAN
FORT, WHICH MEANS 'THE PLACE OF BADGERS'

WALL NORTH DITCH

Brocolitia **A**

LIMESTONE CORNER. THE NORTH DITCH WAS NOT COMPLETED AND THE ROMAN
ENGINEERS APPEAR TO HAVE DOWNED TOOLS IN DISMAY, DESPITE THE FACT
THAT THE VALLUM DITCH WAS COMPLETED – SEE THE NEAT BLOCKS OF
HARD VOLCANIC ROCK LINING THE DITCHES AT THIS POINT

HADRIAN'S WALL AND THE VALLUM
UNUSUALLY CONSTRICT ALONG THE RIDGE

WATERLOGGED PARALLEL VALLUM DITCHES

Limestone Corner **A**

Hadrian scholars numbered the turrets from Wallsend (Segedunum), fitting to the pattern of the Wall's east to west construction. Precisely what the Roman's called each milecastle and turret is not known – it is a great pity that so many lesser Roman names have been lost.

(Dashes show line of Hadrian's Wall Path)

Milecastle 29

Turret 29a

The Military Road descends by Chesters, a Roman cavalry fort – how appropriate that the old stable block opposite is now a stud farm.

Black Carts **L**

Egger's chipboard pulp mill. The white plume helps pin-point Hexham from afar. The steam and smoke are a reminder of the far more invasive industrial fumes that characterised many a town and city in Victorian times, the proverbial 'coals from Newcastle', much of which came from the South Tyne valley and Pennine Fells above Naworth. The alder scrub lining the river is known as 'carr', hence such names as Byker and Walker in Newcastle.

Tyne Bridge, Hexham **L**

This shallow downstream aspect contrasts with the view upstream: an old mill weir gives the impression of a mighty river running alongside the Riverside Park.

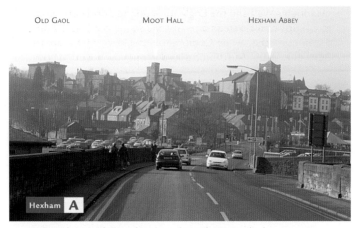

OLD GAOL   MOOT HALL   HEXHAM ABBEY

Hexham **A**

On Sundays and Mondays in July and August lucky passengers have the personal touch of an on-board guide with hands-on Roman replica props, anecdotes and logistical advice. In fact the whole journey is brought vividly life by this team of local experts.

MAKING THE MOST OF YOUR DAY

For many, just to sit and stare while the journey gently unfolds is luxury itself. Yet, the service opens up such wonderful opportunities beyond pure passive apprecia- tion. Why not plan ahead and get involved, experience a moving landscape by visiting the many historic towns, vil- lages and famous sites en route, for there is no compul- sion to stay on board the one bus. The advent of the Hadrian's Wall Path National Trail has added a further dimension to the service, and with an abundance of link- ing paths, you may venture out for a country walk, linking back to a later bus for a refreshing and well-rounded day. Beyond the core service from Carlisle to Hexham given expression in this leaflet, the bus runs the full extent of the Roman frontier from Wallsend to Bowness and back, once a day, enabling the passenger to visit any one point on the Solway/Tyne isthmus.

Hadrian's Wall and the England/Scotland border are often mixed up, even taken as one and the same, but it is a wonderful quirk that while Cumbria by and large trends south from the Wall, Northumberland launches north to give massive scope for fascinating expeditions in a landscape every bit as stunning and rewarding as the immediate environs of the Wall. Just consider that while Carlisle borders Scotland, it is one hundred miles from Newcastle, and much of the space inbetween is a National Park!

South from Brampton runs the heavenly Eden Vale and from Hexham the North Pennine Area of Outstanding Natural Beauty forms the near horizon. This is indeed a blessed area to explore – by bus no less!

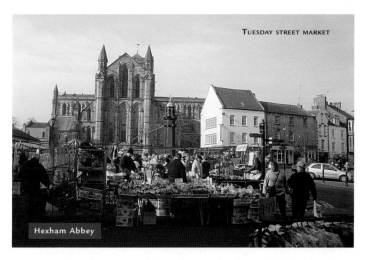

TUESDAY STREET MARKET

Hexham Abbey

The Market Place is a real hive of activity at the heart of a much-loved Tynedale town. Hexham Abbey reflects two phases of construction 1180 to 1250 and 1850 to 1910. Those on a Roman quest will find the Flavius tombstone in the south transept well worth discovering, as too the whole interior of this beautiful priory church.

LISTING OF CICERONE GUIDES

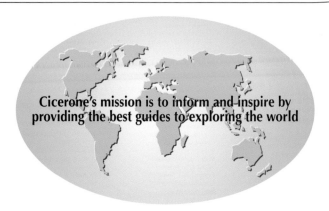

Cicerone's mission is to inform and inspire by
providing the best guides to exploring the world

Since its foundation over 30 years ago, Cicerone has specialised in publishing guidebooks and has built a reputation for quality and reliability. It now publishes nearly 300 guides to the major destinations for outdoor enthusiasts, including Europe, UK and the rest of the world.

Written by leading and committed specialists, Cicerone guides are recognised as the most authoritative. They are full of information, maps and illustrations so that the user can plan and complete a successful and safe trip or expedition – be it a long face climb, a walk over Lakeland fells, an alpine traverse, a Himalayan trek or a ramble in the countryside.

With a thorough introduction to assist planning, clear diagrams, maps and colour photographs to illustrate the terrain and route, and accurate and detailed text, Cicerone guides are designed for ease of use and access to the information.

If the facts on the ground change, or there is any aspect of a guide that you think we can improve, we are always delighted to hear from you.

Cicerone Press
2 Police Square Milnthorpe Cumbria LA7 7PY
Tel:01539 562 069   Fax:01539 563 417
e-mail:info@cicerone.co.uk   web:www.cicerone.co.uk

CICERONE